GAMECUBE
&
GAME BOY® ADVANCE

2005

SECRET CODES

VOLUME 1

GAMECUBE™ GAMES 2

GAME BOY® ADVANCE GAMES 68

//// BRADYGAMES®
TAKE YOUR GAME FURTHER®

Games

1080° AVALANCHE.. 4

4X4 EVOLUTION 2 4

ANIMAL CROSSING 4

BEACH SPIKERS 6

BILLY HATCHER 7

CRASH BANDICOOT: THE WRATH OF CORTEX............................. 10

CUBIX: ROBOTS FOR EVERYONE SHOWDOWN 11

DAKAR 2: THE WORLD'S ULTIMATE RALLY 12

DISNEY'S EXTREME SKATE ADVENTURE..................................... 12

FINDING NEMO 14

FREEKSTYLE 15

THE LEGEND OF ZELDA: WIND WAKER..................................... 18

LOONEY TUNES: BACK IN ACTION 20

MADDEN NFL 2005 20

MARIO GOLF: TOADSTOOL TOUR 23

MEGA MAN ANNIVERSARY COLLECTION 23

MLB SLUGFEST 20-04 27

MVP BASEBALL 2004 30

NASCAR 2005: CHASE FOR THE CUP 30

NASCAR: DIRT TO DAYTONA 34

NBA 2K3 35

NBA LIVE 2003 35

NBA LIVE 2004 35

NBA STREET VOL. 2 38

NCAA FOOTBALL 2005 41

NEED FOR SPEED UNDERGROUND 44

NFL STREET 45

NHL HITZ PRO.. 46

PIKMIN 2 47

PITFALL: THE LOST EXPEDITION 48

SCOOBY-DOO! NIGHT OF 100 FRIGHTS 49

SHREK 2 51

SONIC MEGA COLLECTION 52

SPEED KINGS 54

SSX 3 54

TAK AND THE POWER OF JUJU 59

TEENAGE MUTANT NINJA TURTLES 60

TIGER WOODS PGA TOUR 2004 61

TIGER WOODS PGA TOUR 2005 62

TY THE TASMANIAN TIGER 67

WHIRL TOUR 67

YU-GI-OH! FALSEBOUND KINGDOM 67

1080° AVALANCHE

Select Enter An Avalanche Code from the Options, and enter the following codes:

NOVICE AVALANCHE CHALLENGE
Enter JAS3IKRR.

HARD AVALANCHE CHALLENGE
Enter 2AUNIKFS.

EXPERT AVALANCHE CHALLENGE
Enter EATFIKRM.

EXTREME AVALANCHE CHALLENGE
Enter 9AVVIKNY.

4X4 EVOLUTION 2

LEVEL SELECT
At the title screen, press X, X, Z, Z, Y, Y, Z, X, Y, Y, X, Z.

EXTRA MONEY
At the title screen, press Y, X, Z, Y, X, Z, X, X, Y, Z, X, Y.

INCREASE REPUTATION
At the title screen, press Y, Y, Z, X, X, Z, Y (x3), X (x3).

ANIMAL CROSSING

TOM NOOK PASSWORDS
Talk to Tom Nook and select Other Things. Then, select Say code and enter the following passwords. You will only be able to enter 3 at a time.

PASSWORD	ITEM
CbDahLBdaDh98d 9ub8ExzZKwu7Zl	Balloon Fight NES Game
1n5%N%8JUjE5fj lEcGr4%ync5eUp	Baseball NES Game
Crm%h4BNRyu98d 9uu8exzZKwu7Zl	Clu Clu Land NES Game
bA5PC%8JUjE5fj ljcGr4%ync5EUp	DK Jr. Math NES Game
2n5@N%8JUjE5fj ljcGr4%ync5EUp	Donkey Kong NES Game
3%Q4fhMTRByAY3 05yYAK9zNHxLd7	Excitebike NES Game
Crm%h4BNRbu98d 9un8exzZKwo7Zl	Golf NES Game
bA5PC%8JUjE5fj 1EcGr4%ync5eup	Wario's Woods NES Game
Wn2&SAVAcgIC7N POudE2Tk8JHyUH	10,000 Bells from Project Hyrule
WB2&pARAcnOwnU jMCK%hTk8JHyrT	30,000 Bells from Project Hyrule

PASSWORD	ITEM
#SbaUIRmw#gwkY BK66q#LGscTY%2	? Block
IboOBCeHz3YbIC B5igPvQYsfMZMd	Block Flooring
1mWYg6IfB@&q75 8XzSNKpfWj76ts	Brick Block
4UT6T6L89ZnOW3 dw&%jtL3qjLZBf	Cannon
4UT6T948GZnOW3 dw#%jtLEqj5ZBf	Fire Flower
4UT6T6L89ZnOW3 dwU%jtL3qjLZBf	Flagpole
1mWYg6IfB@&q7z 8XzSNwpfij76ts	Green Pipe
BCQ4iZFK%i5xqo SnyrjcrwAeDMkQ	Luigi Trophy
QI6DLEnhm23CqH zrUHk3cXd#HOr9	Mushroom Mural
4UF6T948GZ3ZW3 dw#%jtLEqj5ZBf	Starman
1LhOwvrDA23fmt dsgnvzbCIBAsyd	Station Model 1

LETTER TO VILLAGER PASSWORDS

For the following passwords, send the password to one of the animals living in your town. Only include the password in the body of the letter. Be sure to include a line break between the two lines of code.

PASSWORD	ITEM
rSbaUIRmwUgwkA1K6tq#LMscTY%2	Coin
rSbaUIAmwUgwkY1K6tq#LGscTY%2	Koopa Shell
ECzihy%rtHbHuko3XIP3IslEqI#K	Mario Trophy
#SbaUIRmw#gwkYBh66qeLMscTY%2	Super Mushroom

BEACH SPIKERS

UNIFORMS

In World Tour, name your player one of the following to unlock bonus outfits. The name disappears when entered correctly.

NAME	UNIFORMS
JUSTICE	105-106
	Sunglasses 94
DAYTONA	107-108
FVIPERS	109-110
	Face 51
	Hair 75
ARAKATA	111-113
	Face 52
	Hair 76

NAME	UNIFORMS
PHANTA2	114-115
	Face 53
	Hair 77
OHTORII	116-117

BILLY HATCHER

SEGA EGG ANIMALS

On your plight to save Morning Land from the Crows, you'll discover eight opaque eggs. Printed on these eggs is a blue Sonic Hedgehog head. When you collect the right amount of Chick Coins, these eggs can be rolled, fed, and hatched. Inside these eggs are well-known characters from popular Sega games. Unfortunately, they can only be found and used in the Mission where there egg is found, just like any Egg Animal.

SEGA EGG ANIMALS

EGG #	HATCH	DESCRIPTION	EGG LOCATION
56	Sonic	From *Sonic DX*	Dino Mountain 3
57	Tails	From *Sonic DX*	Sand Ruin 5
58	Knuckles	From *Sonic DX*	Forest Village 8
59	Chao	From *Chao Adventure*	Forest Village 1
60	Rappy	From *Phantasy Star Online*	Blizzard Castle 2
61	Kapu Kapu	From *Chu Chu Rocket*	Pirates Island 5
62	NiGHTS	From *NiGHTS Into Dreams*	Giant Palace 4
63	Amigo	From *Samba De Amigo*	Circus Park 4

Sonic

Sonic zips around defeating anything he touches and bounces off walls to continue his rampage in a new direction.

Tails

Tails soars through the air and behaves similarly to a boomerang. Once you aim him at an enemy, you can move so that Tails' return trajectory puts him on a collision course with more enemies.

Knuckles

Knuckles is amazing! He zips around at blinding speed, devastating anything in his zig-zagging path. He even leaves the ground to attack airborne Crows, such as those flying infuriating menaces the Beens!

Chao

Chao's attack style is a water bubble that mows down anyone in its path and ends with a large splash that consumes anyone within range.

Rappy

Rappy quickly zips along the ground in short bursts of speed, rests, and then zips off towards the closest enemy. He seeks out enemies to destroy.

Kapu Kapu

Kapu Kapu bounces off walls, sending him chomping in a new direction. He won't hunt down enemies, so use him in small areas crowded with enemies.

Nights

Nights flies much more quickly, making it easier for bouncing enemies to evade her flyby attack. Releasing her in a room full of Big Doras is lethal.

Amigo

Amigo can slice through and destroy a Larpee as he's spinning! He's deadly with those maracas.

CRASH BANDICOOT: THE WRATH OF CORTEX

ALL LEVELS AND ALL GEMS

Enter **wombat** as your name.

CUBIX: ROBOTS FOR EVERYONE SHOWDOWN

Select Cheats from the Extras menu and enter the following:

COMPLETE GAME AS ABBY
Press X, R, X, Y, X, Y, R, L.

COMPLETE GAME AS CONNOR
Press X, Y, L, Y, X, Y, L, R.

DR. K'S BASE ROBOTS
Press Z, A, Y (x3), X, A.

CONSTRUCTION ROBOTS
Press Y (x4), Z, A, R.

BUBBLE TOWN DAY ROBOTS
Press Y, Y, Z, Y, Y, R, L.

BUBBLE TOWN NIGHT ROBOTS
Press Y, L, Y, Y, X, L, Z.

DAKAR 2: THE WORLD'S ULTIMATE RALLY

Select Cheat Code from the Extras menu and enter the following:

ALL VEHICLES
Enter SWEETAS.

ALL TRACKS
Enter BONZER.

DISNEY'S EXTREME SKATE ADVENTURE

Select Cheat Codes from the Options and enter the following:

ALL LEVELS
Enter ambassador.

ALL SKATERS
Enter entourage.

ALL CREATE-A-SKATER ITEMS
Enter trendytrickster.

SPECIAL METER ALWAYS FULL
Enter inthezone.

LION KING VIDEO
Enter savannah.

TOY STORY VIDEO
Enter marin.

TARZAN VIDEO
Enter nugget.

FINDING NEMO

Enter the following at the main menu. The word Cheat! will appear if entered correctly. Pause the game at the Level select to access the cheats.

LEVEL SELECT
Press Y (x3), B, B, X, B, Y, X, B, Y, B, Y, B, Y, X, Y, Y.

INVINCIBILITY
Press Y, B, B, X (x3), Y, Y, B (x3), X (x4), B, Y, X (x3), B,X, Y,X, X, B, X, X, Y, X, B, X (x3), Y.

CREDITS
Press Y, B, X, Y, Y, B, X, Y, B, X, Y, B, B, X, Y, B, X, Y, B, X, X, Y, B, X.

SECRET LEVEL

Press Y, B, X, X, B, Y, Y, B, X, X, B, Y, Y, X, B, Y, B, X, X, B, Y.

FREEKSTYLE

Select Enter Codes from the Options screen and enter the following:

ALL CHARACTERS, OUTFITS, BIKES, AND LEVELS
Enter **LOKSMITH**.

ALL CHARACTERS
Enter **POPULATE**.

ALL COSTUMES
Enter **YARDSALE**.

ALL BIKES
Enter **WHEELS**.

ALL TRACKS
Enter **TRAKMEET**.

CLIFFORD ADOPTANTE
Enter **COOLDUDE**.

MIKE JONES
Enter **TOUGHGUY**.

JESSICA PATTERSON
Enter **BLONDIE**.

GREG ALBERTYN
Enter **GIMEGREG**.

UNLIMITED FREEKOUT
Enter **ALLFREEK**.

QUICKER FREEKOUT METER
Enter **FIRESALE**.

LAND A TRICK FOR A FULL BOOST
Enter **MO BOOST**.

INFINITE BOOST
Enter **FREEBIE**.

NO BIKE
Enter **FLYSOLO**.

RIDER WEARS A HELMET
Enter **HELMET**.

LOW GRAVITY
Enter **FTAIL**.

SLOW MOTION
Enter **WTCHKPRS**.

BURN IT UP TRACK
Enter **CARVEROK**.

GNOME SWEET GNOME TRACK
Enter **CLIPPERS**.

LET IT RIDE TRACK
Enter **BLACKJAK**.

ROCKET GARDEN TRACK
Enter **TODAMOON**.

CRASH PAD FREESTYLE TRACK
Enter **WIDEOPEN**.

BURBS FREESTYLE TRACK
Enter **TUCKELLE**.

BIKES

Enter the following codes to access to different bikes:

CHARACTER	BIKE	CODE
Mike Metzger	Bloodshot	EYEDROPS
	Rock Of Ages	BRRRRRAP
	Rhino Rage	SEVENTWO
Brian Deegan	Mulisha Man	WHATEVER
	Heavy Metal	HEDBANGR
	Dominator	WHOZASKN
Leeann Tweeden	Hot Stuff	OVENMITT
	Trendsetter	STYLIN
	Seducer	GOODLOOK
Stefy Bau	Amore	HEREIAM
	Disco Tech	SPARKLES
	211	TWONEONE
Clifford Adoptante	Gone Tiki	SUPDUDE
	Island Spirit	GOFLOBRO
	Hang Loose	STOKED
Mike Jones	Beater	KICKBUTT
	Lil' Demon	HORNS
	Flushed	PLUNGER
Jessica Patterson	Speedy	HEKACOOL
	Charged Up	LIGHTNIN
	Racer Girl	TONBOY
Greg Albertyn	The King	ALLSHOOK
	National Pride	PATRIOT
	Champion	NUMBER

OUTFITS

Enter the following to access different outfits:

CHARACTER	OUTFIT	CODE
Mike Metzger	Ecko MX	HELLOOOO
	All Tatted Up	BODYART
Brian Deegan	Muscle Bound	RIPPED
	Commander	SOLDIER
Leeann Tweeden	Fun Lovin'	THNKPINK
	Red Hot	SPICY
Stefy Bau	Playing Jax	KIDSGAME
	UFO Racer	INVASION

CHARACTER	OUTFIT	CODE
Clifford Adoptante	Tiki	WINGS
	Tankin' It	NOSLEEVE
Mike Jones	Blue Collar	BABYBLUE
	High Roller	BOXCARS
Jessica Patterson	Warming Up	LAYERS
	Hoodie Style	NOT2GRLY
Greg Albertyn	Sharp Dresser	ILOOKGUD
	Star Rider	COMET

THE LEGEND OF ZELDA: WIND WAKER

GAME COMPLETION BONUSES

Be sure to save your game to an empty file after completing it. There are numerous bonuses available for those who decide to play through the game a second time.

Link's Pajamas

Link doesn't receive the Hero's Clothes from Grandma. Instead, he wears his blue pajamas throughout the adventure.

Aryll's Skull Dress

Aryll wears the purple "skull" dress throughout the game. She is given this dress while in Forsaken Fortress.

Deluxe Picto-Box

Link starts his new adventure with the Deluxe Picto Box. Now he can take color pictographs right from the start!

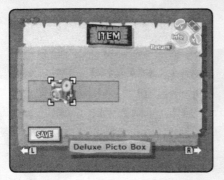

Nintendo Gallery

If Link started his figurine collection in the first play-through, have no fear! All of the figurines, as well as the film in the Deluxe Picto-Box, will carry over to the second game save.

Hylian to English

All of the text that appeared in the indecipherable Hylian language during the first play-through will now be displayed in English. Now Link can see what Jabun, Valoo, and the Great Deku Tree were saying about him!

LOONEY TUNES: BACK IN ACTION

LEVEL SELECT
Enter PASSPORT as a code.

INVINCIBLE
Enter TOUGHAGE as a code.

CANNON BALL COSTUME
Enter CANNON as a code.

DUCK DANGER COSTUME
Enter DANGERD as a code.

ADDITIONAL $500
Enter AMUNKEY as a code.

FREE COSTUME DOORS
Enter SUITSYOU as a code.

GOSSAMER DOORS IN THE WARNER BROS. STUDIOS
Enter GOBBLE as a code.

HEN GRENADES
Enter HENSAWAY as a code.

SLAPPY FISH
Enter SLAPPY as a code.

ACME SHRINK RAY
Enter WEENY as a code.

DUCK DANGER BATTLE
Enter OUTTAKE as a code.

WILE. E. COYOTE MINI-GAME
Enter FURRYOUS as a code.

MADDEN NFL 2005

MADDEN CARD CODES
Select Madden Cards from the My Madden menu. Then, select Madden Codes and enter the following:

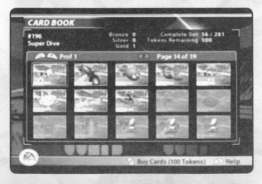

CODE	CARD	DESCRIPTION
P67E1I	TJ Duckett	Gold TJ Duckett
Z28X8K	3rd Down	For 1 Half, your opponent will only get 3 downs to get a first down
P66C4L	5th Down	For 1 Half, you will get 5 downs to get a first down
J33I8F	Bingo!	Your defensive interceptions increase by 75% for the game
B61A8M	Da Bomb	You will receive unlimited pass range for 1 Half
I76X3T	Da Boot	You will receive unlimited field goal range for 1 Half
M89S8G	Extra Credit	Awards 4 points for every interception and 3 points for every sack
V65J8P	First and Fifteen	Requires your opponent to get 15 yards to reach a first down for 1 Half
O72E9B	First and Five	Your first down yards to go will be set to 5 for 1 Half
R14B8Z	Fumblitis	Your opponent's fumbles will increase by 75% for the game
L96J7P	Human Plow	Your Broken Tackles will increases by 75% for the game
D57R5S	Lame Duck	Your opponent will throw a lob pass for 1 Half
X78P9Z	Mistake Free	You can't fumble or throw an interception for 1 Half
Y59R8R	Mr. Mobility	Your QB can't get sacked for 1 Half
D59K3Y	Super Dive	Your diving distance increases by 75% for the game
V34L6D	Tight Fit	Your opponent's uprights will be made very narrow for 1 Half
L48G1E	Unforced Errors	Your opponent will fumble every time he tries to juke for 1 Half

MARIO GOLF: TOADSTOOL TOUR

At the title screen, press Start + Z to open the password screen. Enter the following to open up bonus tournaments:

TARGET BULLSEYE TOURNAMENT
Enter CEUFPXJ1.

HOLLYWOOD VIDEO TOURNAMENT
Enter BJGQBULZ.

CAMP HYRULE TOURNAMENT
Enter 0EKW5G7U.

BOWSER BADLANDS TOURNAMENT
Enter 9L3L9KHR.

BOWSER JR.'S JUMBO TOURNAMENT
Enter 2GPL67PN.

MARIO OPEN TOURNAMENT
Enter GGAA241H.

PEACH'S INVITATIONAL TOURNAMENT
Enter ELBUT3PX.

MEGA MAN ANNIVERSARY COLLECTION

Mega Man 2

VILLAIN DEFEAT PASSWORDS

Flash Man	A2, C1, C2, C5, D3, E1, E2, E3
Wood Man	A2, C2, C4, C5, D3, D4, E1, E2, E3
Air Man	A2, C2, C4, C5, D4, E1, E2, E3, E4
Metal Man	A4, B1, B3, C4, D1, D2, E1, E3, E4
Bubble Man	A4, B1, B3, C4, D2, D4, E1, E3, E4
Crash Man	A4, B1, B3, C4, D2, D3, D4, E1, E3
Heat Man	A1, B2, C1, C4, C5, D1, D3, E3, E5
Quick Man	A2, B1, B3, B5, C2, D1, D2, D4, E4

START GAME WITH FOUR E-TANKS

A5, B1, B3, C4, D2, D3, E1, E5

HALF OF GAME COMPLETE: AIR MAN, BUBBLE MAN, CRASH MAN, FLASH MAN, AND FOUR E-TANKS

A5, B2, C4, C5, D3, D4, D5, E4, E5

HALF OF GAME COMPLETE: HEAT MAN, METAL MAN, QUICK MAN, WOOD MAN, AND FOUR E-TANKS

A5, B1, B4, C1, C3, D2, E1, E2

ALL WEAPONS

A5 B2 B4 C1 C3 C5 D4 D5 E2

LONG JUMPS

Pause in the middle of a jump to reset Mega Man's downward velocity. Press Start rapidly at the height of a jump to coast for long distances. This also makes most bullets fly through Mega Man without harm.

START WITH ALL BOSSES DEFEATED AT WILEY'S CASTLE

A1 B2 B4 C1 C5 D1 D3 E3 E5

START WITH ALL BOSSES DEFEATED AT WILEY'S CASTLE & 4 ENERGY TANKS

A5 B2 B4 C1 C3 C5 D4 D5 E2

Mega Man 3

ALL WEAPONS/ALL ITEMS/9 ETs/0 DOC ROBOTS

Blue: A3 B5 D3 F4

Red: A6

ALL WEAPONS/ALL ITEMS/9 ETs/DR. WILEY STAGE 1

Blue: A1 A3 B2 B5 D3 F4

Red: A6 E1

SPARK MAN DEFEATED

Red: C5, F4

SNAKE MAN DEFEATED

Red: C5, F6

NEEDLE MAN DEFEATED

Red: D3, E6

HARD MAN DEFEATED

Red: C4, E6

TOP MAN DEFEATED

Red: A3, C5

GEMINI MAN DEFEATED

Red: B5, C5

MAGNET MAN DEFEATED

Red: C5, F5

SHADOW MAN DEFEATED

Red: C5, D6

Mega Man 4

ALL WEAPONS AND ITEMS
A1, A4, B5, E2, F1, F3

BRIGHT MAN DEFEATED
A1, A4, B5, E2, F1, F3

DIVE MAN DEFEATED
A2, B4, B5, D2, E2, F3

DRILL MAN DEFEATED
A2, A4, B5, E2, E4, F3

PHARAOH MAN DEFEATED
A2, A5, B2, B4, D1, D3

RING MAN DEFEATED
A2, B3, B4, B5, D1, D3

SKULL MAN
A2, B4, B5, C4, D3, F2

TOAD MAN DEFEATED
A4, B1, B5, E2, E6, F3

Mega Man 5

ALL WEAPONS AND ITEMS
Blue: B4 D6 F1
Red: C1 D4 F6

CHARGE MAN DEFEATED
Red: C1, D4, F6
Blue: B4, D6, F1

CRYSTAL MAN DEFEATED
Red: A5, D2, E3
Blue: B1, B3, E5

DR. WILEY'S LAIR
Red: C1, D4, F6
Blue: B4, D6, F1

GRAVITY MAN DEFEATED
Red: A5, B1, F4
Blue: C4, E5, F1

GYRO MAN DEFEATED
Red: A5, B1, E3
Blue: B3, E5, F1

NAPALM MAN DEFEATED
Red: A5, C1, E3
Blue: B3, E2, E5

STAR MAN DEFEATED
Red: B1, B6, F4
Blue: C4, E6, F1

STONE MAN DEFEATED
Red: C1, E3, F6
Blue: B3, D6, E2

WAVE MAN DEFEATED
Red: B1, B6, D3
Blue: B3, E6, F1

EXTRA CONTINUES
Get the energy tank on the first level of Dr. Wiley's Castle. Then get killed, and Continue the game. You can do this until you have 9 Continues.

M TANK & 1UP TRICK
If you have an M Tank, full energy, all weapons, pause the game and use an M tank. All enemies will turn into 1Ups. This does not work on bosses!

Mega Man 6

ALL WEAPONS AND ITEMS
B6 D4 F2 F4 F6

Mega Man 7

ALL WEAPONS AND ITEMS
7 2 5 1 5 8 4 2 2 8 4 7 6 1 3 7

FINAL STAGE
1415 5585 7823 6251

FINAL STAGE/ALL ITEMS/999 BOLTS/4 ENERGY TANKS/4 WEAPON TANKS
7853-5842-2245-7515

Mega Man 8

ANIMATION TEST
Choose Bonus Mode, hold down L + R, and press Start.

MLB SLUGFEST 20-04

CHEATS

At the Match-Up screen, use B, Y, and X to enter the following codes, and press the appropriate direction. For example, for Alien Team (231 Down) press B two times, Y three times, X one time, and then press Down.

CODE	ENTER
Cheats Disabled	111 Down
Unlimited Turbo	444 Down
No Fatigue	343 Up
No Contact Mode	433 Left
16' Softball	242 Down

CODE	ENTER
Rubber Ball	242 Up
Whiffle Bat	004 Right
Blade Bat	002 Up
Bone Bat	001 Up
Ice Bat	003 Up
Log Bat	004 Up
Mace Bat	004 Left
Spike Bat	005 Up
Big Head	200 Right
Tiny Head	200 Left
Max Batting	300 Left
Max Power	030 Left
Max Speed	003 Left
Alien Team	231 Down
Bobble Head Team	133 Down

CODE	ENTER
Casey Team	233 Down
Dolphin Team	102 Down
Dwarf Team	103 Down
Eagle Team	212 Right
Evil Clown Team	211 Down
Gladiator Team	113 Down
Horse Team	211 Right

CODE	ENTER
Lion Team	220 Right
Little League	101 Down
Minotaur Team	110 Down
Napalitano Team	232 Down

CODE	ENTER
Olshan Team	222 Down
Pinto Team	210 Right
Rivera Team	222 Up
Rodeo Clown	132 Down
Scorpion Team	112 Down
Team Terry Fitzgerald	333 Right
Team Todd McFarlane	222 Right
Atlantis Stadium	321 Left
Coliseum Stadium	333 Up

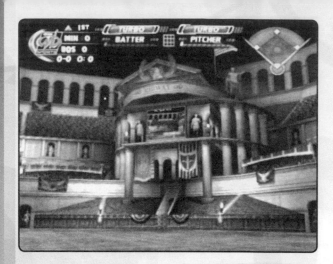

CODE	ENTER
Empire Park Stadium	321 Right
Forbidden City Stadium	333 Left
Midway Park Stadium	321 Down
Monument Stadium	333 Down
Rocket Park Stadium	321 Up
Extended Time for Codes	303 Up

MVP BASEBALL 2004

THIN BAT
Create a player with the name Erik Kiss.

BIG BAT
Create a player with the name Jacob Paterson.

BIG CAP
Create a player with the name John Prosen.

NASCAR 2005: CHASE FOR THE CUP

ALL BONUSES
At the Edit Driver screen, enter Open Sesame as your name.

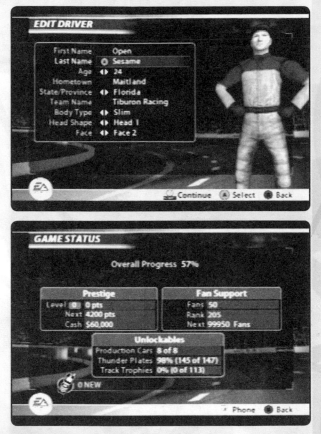

DALE EARNHARDT

At the Edit Driver screen, enter The Intimidator as your name.

$10,000,000

At the Edit Driver screen, enter Walmart NASCAR as your name.

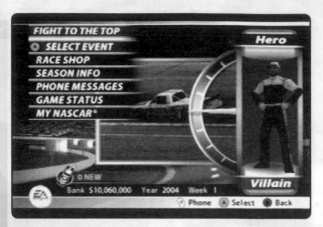

LAKESHORE DRIVE TRACK

At the Edit Driver screen, enter Walmart Exclusive as your name.

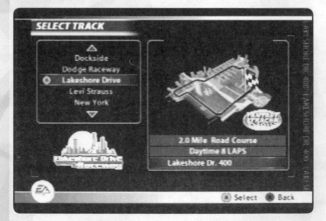

DODGE EVENTS

At the Edit Driver screen, enter Dodge Stadium as your name.

MR CLEAN DRIVERS

At the Edit Driver screen, enter Mr.Clean Racing as your name.

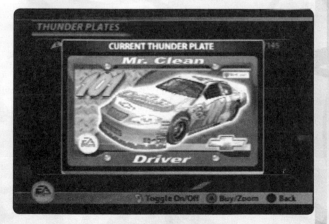

MR. CLEAN PIT CREW

At the Edit Driver screen, enter Clean Crew as your name.

2,000,000 PRESTIGE POINTS/LEVEL 10 IN FIGHT TO THE TOP MODE

At the Edit Driver screen, enter You TheMan as your name.

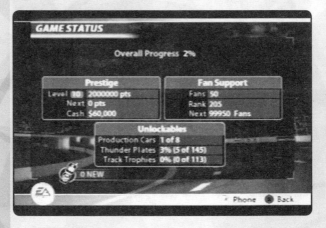

NASCAR: DIRT TO DAYTONA

$10,000

At the Main Menu, press Up, Down, Left, Right, Z, Left, Left.

NBA 2K3

Select Game Play from the Options menu. Hold Left on the D-pad + Right on the Left Analog Stick, and press Start. Exit to the Options menu, and the Codes option will appear.

SEGA SPORTS, VISUAL CONCEPTS, AND NBA 2K3 TEAMS

Enter MEGASTARS as a code.

STREET TRASH

Enter SPRINGER as a code.

DUOTONE DRAW

Enter DUOTONE as a code.

NBA LIVE 2003

Create a player with the following last names. These characters will be available as free agents:

B-RICH

Enter DOLLABILLS.

BUSTA RHYMES

Enter FLIPMODE.

DJ CLUE

Enter MIXTAPES.

GHETTO FABULOUS

Enter GHETTOFAB.

HOT KARL

Enter CALIFORNIA.

JUST BLAZE

Enter GOODBEATS.

NBA LIVE 2004

Create a player with the following last name. The player will be placed in Free Agents:

ALEKSANDER PAVLOVIC

Enter WHSUCPOI.

ANDREAS GLYNIADAKIS

Enter POCKDLEK.

CARLOS DELFINO

Enter SDFGURKL.

JAMES LANG
Enter NBVKSMCN.

JERMAINE DUPRI
Enter SOSODEF.

KYLE KORVER
Enter OEISNDLA.

MALICK BADIANE
Enter SKENXIDO.

MARIO AUSTIN
Enter POSNEGHX.

MATT BONNER
Enter BBVDKCVM.

NEDZAD SINANOVIC
Enter ZXDSDRKE.

PACCELIS MORLENDE
Enter QWPOASZX.

REMON VAN DE HARE
Enter ITNVCJSD.

RICK RICKERT
Enter POILKJMN.

SANI BECIROVIC
Enter ZXCCVDRI.

SOFOKLIS SCHORTSANITIS
Enter IOUBFDCJ.

SZYMON SZEWCZYK
Enter POIOIJIS.

TOMMY SMITH
Enter XCFWQASE.

XUE YUYANG
Enter WMZKCOI.

Select NBA Codes from the My NBA LIVE option and enter the following:

15,000 NBA STORE POINTS
Enter 87843H5F9P.

ALL HARDWOOD CLASSIC JERSEYS
Enter 725JKUPLMM.

ALL NBA GEAR
Enter ERT9976KJ3.

ALL TEAM GEAR
Enter YREY5625WQ.

ALL SHOES
Enter POUY985GY5.

UNLOCK SHOES

Select My NBA Live and enter the following NBA Codes to unlock the different shoes:

SHOES	CODE
Air Bounds (black/white/blue)	7YSS0292KE
Air Bounds (white/black)	JA807YAM20
Air Bounds (white/green)	84HHST61QI
Air Flight 89 (black/white)	FG874JND84
Air Flight 89 (white/black)	63RBVC7423
Air Flight 89 (white/red)	GF9845JHR4
Air Flightposite 2 (blue/gray)	2389JASE3E
Air Flightposite (white/black/gray)	74FDH7K94S
Air Flightposite (white/black)	6HJ874SFJ7
Air Flightposite (yellow/black/white)	MN54BV45C2
Air Flightposite 2 (blue/gray)	RB84UJHAS2
Air Flightposite 2 (blue/gray)	2389JASE3E
Air Foamposite 1 (blue)	OP5465UX12
Air Foamposite 1 (white/black/red)	D0D843HH7F
Air Foamposite Pro (blue/black)	DG56TRF446
Air Foamposite Pro (black/gray)	3245AFSD45
Air Foamposite Pro (red/black)	DSAKF38422
Air Force Max (black)	F84N845H92
Air Force Max (white/black/blue)	985KJF98KJ
Air Force Max (white/red)	8734HU8FFF
Air Hyperflight (white)	14TGU7DEWC
Air Hyperflight (black/white)	WW44YHU592
Air Hyperflight (blue/white)	A0K374HF8S
Air Hyperflight (yellow/black)	JCX93LSS88
Air Jordan 11 (black/red/white)	GF64H76ZX5
Air Jordan 11 (black/varsity royal/white)	HJ987RTGFA
Air Jordan 11 (cool grey)	GF75HG6332
Air Jordan 11 (white)	HG76HN765S
Air Jordan 11 (white/black)	A2S35TH7H6
Air Jordan 3 (white)	G9845HJ8F4
Air Jordan 3 (white/clay)	435SGF555Y
Air Jordan 3 (white/fire red)	RE6556TT90

SHOES	CODE
Air Jordan 3 (white/true blue)	FDS9D74J4F
Air Jordan 3 (black/white/gray)	CVJ554TJ58
Air Max2 CB (black/white)	87HZXGFIU8
Air Max2 CB (white/red)	4545GFKJIU
Air Max2 Uptempo (black/white/blue)	NF8745J87F
Air Max Elite (black)	A4CD54T7TD
Air Max Elite (white/black)	966ERTFG65
Air Max Elite (white/blue)	FD9KN48FJF
Air Zoom Flight (gray/white)	367UEY6SN
Air Zoom Flight (white/blue)	92387HDO77
Zoom Generation (white/black/red)	23LBJNUMB1
Zoom Generation (black/red/white)	LBJ23CAVS1
Nike Blazer (khaki)	W3R57U9NB2
Nike Blazer (tan/white/blue)	DCT5YHMU90
Nike Blazer (white/orange/blue)	4G66JU99XS
Nike Blazer (black)	XCV6456NNL
Nike Shox BB4 (black)	WE424TY563
Nike Shox BB4 (white/black)	23ERT85LP9
Nike Shox BB4 (white/light purple)	668YYTRB12
Nike Shox BB4 (white/red)	424TREU777
Nike Shox VCIII (black)	SDFH764FJU
Nike Shox VCIII (white/black/red)	5JHD367JJT

NBA STREET VOL. 2

Select Pick Up Game, hold L, and enter the following when "Enter cheat codes now" appears at the bottom of the screen:

UNLIMITED TURBO
Press B, B, Y, Y.

ABA BALL
Press X, B, X, B.

WNBA BALL
Press X, Y, Y, X.

NO DISPLAY BARS
Press B, X (x3).

ALL JERSEYS
Press X, Y, B, B.

ALL COURTS
Press B, Y, Y, B.

ST. LUNATICS TEAM AND ALL STREET LEGENDS
Press X, Y, B, Y.

ALL NBA LEGENDS
Press X, Y, Y, B.

CLASSIC MICHAEL JORDAN
Press X, Y, X, X.

EXPLOSIVE RIMS
Press X (x3), Y.

BIG HEADS
Press X, B, B, X.

SMALL PLAYERS

Press Y, Y, X, B.

NO COUNTERS

Press Y, Y, X, X.

BALL TRAILS

Press Y, Y, Y, B.

ALL QUICKS

Press Y, X, Y, B.

EASY SHOTS

Press Y, X, B, Y.

HARD SHOTS

Press Y, B, X, Y.

NCAA FOOTBALL 2005

PENNANT CODES

Select My NCAA and then Pennant Collection. Enter the following Pennant Codes:

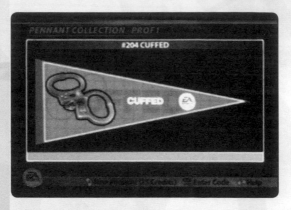

PENNANT COLLECTION PROF 1

#204 CUFFED

CUFFED

CODE	EFFECT
Thanks	1st and 15
For	Blink Cheat
Registering	Boing (dropped passes)
Tiburon	Crossed The Line Cheat
EA Sports	Cuffed Cheat
Hike	Jumbalaya Cheat
Home Field	Molasses Cheat
Elite 11	QB Dud Cheat
NCAA	Stiffed Cheat
Football	Take Your Time Cheat
2005	Thread The Needle Cheat
Blitz	What a Hit Cheat
Sic Em	Baylor ratings boost
Oskee Wow	Illinois ratings boost
Fight	Texas Tech ratings boost

CODE	EFFECT
Fumble	2003 All-Americans
Roll Tide	All-Alabama
WooPigSooie	All-Arkansas
War Eagle	All-Auburn
Death Valley	All-Clemson
Glory	All-Colorado
Great To Be	All-Florida
Uprising	All-FSU
Hunker Down	All-Georgia
On Iowa	All-Iowa
Victory	All-Kansas State
Geaux Tigers	All-LSU
Hail State	All-Mississippi State
Raising Cane	All-Miami
Go Blue	All-Michigan
Go Big Red	All-Nebraska
Rah Rah	All-North Carolina
Golden Domer	All-Notre Dame
Killer Nuts	All-Ohio State
Boomer	All-Oklahoma
Go Pokes	All-Oklahoma State
Quack Attack	All-Oregon
We Are	All-Penn State
Lets Go Pitt	All-Pittsburgh
Boiler Up	All-Purdue
Orange Crush	All-Syracuse
Big Orange	All-Tennessee
Hook Em	All-Texas
Gig Em	All-Texas A&M
Mighty	All-UCLA
Fight On	All-USC
Wahoos	All-Virginia
Tech Triumph	All-Virginia Tech
Bow Down	All-Washington
U Rah Rah	All-Wisconsin
Bear Down	Arizona Mascot Team
Ramblinwreck	Georgia Tech Mascot Team

CODE	EFFECT
Red And Gold	Iowa State Mascot Team
Rock Chalk	Kansas Mascot Team
On On UK	Kentucky Mascot Team
Go Green	Michigan State Mascot Team
Rah Rah Rah	Minnesota Mascot Team
Mizzou Rah	Missouri Mascot Team
Go Pack	North Carolina State Mascot Team
Go Cats	Northwestern Mascot Team
Hotty Totty	Ole Miss Mascot Team
Hail WV	West Virginia Mascot Team
Go Deacs Go	Wake Forest Mascot Team
All Hail	Washington State Mascot Team

NEED FOR SPEED UNDERGROUND

ALL CIRCUIT TRACKS
At the main menu, press Down, R (x3), X (x3), Z.

ALL DRAG TRACKS
At the main menu, press Right, Z, Left, R, Z, L, Y, X.

ALL DRIFT TRACKS
At the main menu, press Left (x4), Right, X, R, Y.

ALL SPRINT TRACKS
At the main menu, press Up, X (x3), R, Down (x3).

DRIFT PHYSICS
At the main menu, press R, Up (x3), Down (x3), L.

NFL STREET

FIELDS AND TEAMS

Enter the following as your user ID:

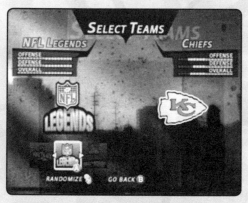

USER ID	UNLOCK
Travel	All Fields
Classic	NFL Legends
Excellent	X-ecutioner Team
AW9378	Divisional All-Star Teams

NFL Legends code.

All Fields code.

Division All-Star Teams code.

NHL HITZ PRO

At the Select Teams screen, select User and enter the following:

BIG PLAYER HEAD
Enter HERK.

BIG TEAM HEADS
Enter INGY.

DIFFERENT PUCK SIZE
Enter 211S.

DIFFERENT PUCK SHADOW
Enter SASG.

PUCK GLOWS
Enter CARB.

PIKMIN 2

TITLE SCREEN

At the title screen, use the following controls:

Press R to make the Pikmin form NINTENDO.

Press L to go back to PIKMIN 2.

Press X to get a beetle.

Use the C-Stick to move it around.

Press L to get rid of the Beetle.

Press Y to get a Chappie.

Use the C-Stick to move it around.

Press Z to eat the Pikmin.

Press L to get rid of Chappie.

© 2004 Nintendo

PITFALL: THE LOST EXPEDITION

PLAY AS NICOLE

At the title screen, hold L + R and press Left, Up, Down, Up, X, Up, Up.

INFINITE WATER IN CANTEEN

At the title screen, hold L + R and press Left, B, X, Down, B, A, B, X.

HYPER PUNCH MODE

At the title screen, hold L + R and press Left, Right, X, Up, X, Right, Left.

CLASSIC PITFALL

At the title screen, hold L + R and press X, X, Left, Right, X, B, A, Up, X.

CLASSIC PITFALL 2: LOST CAVERNS

At the title screen, hold L + R and press Left, Right, Left, Right, Y (x3).

SCOOBY-DOO! NIGHT OF 100 FRIGHTS

ALL POWER-IPS

Pause the game, hold L + R, and press X, B, X, B, X, B, X, B, B, B, X, X, B, X, X, X.

ALL WARP GATES

Pause the game, hold L + R, and press B, B, X, B, B, X, B, X (x3).

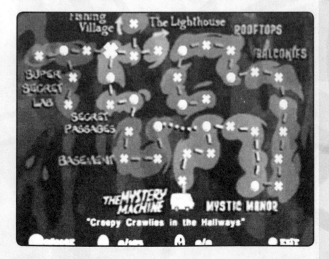

ALL MOVIES

Pause the game, hold L + R, and press B (x3), X (x3), B, X, B.

ALTERNATE CREDITS

Pause the game, hold L + R, and press B, X, X, B, X, B.

HOLIDAYS

January 1
July 4
October 31
December 25

SHREK 2

UNLOCK LEVELS

Enter the first level, and press the Start button. Enter Scrapbook from the in-game Pause Menu. Enter the following code 3 times on the D-Pad: Left, Up, A, X. Then press Up 5 times on the D-Pad. When done correctly you will hear a voice announce, "That's what I call spreading joy."

Exit out of the menu using the B Button. Select Exit Level and choose Yes to confirm your choice. Select Chapter Select on the Contents menu to view and select the unlock levels.

UNLOCK BONUS GAMES

Enter any level, and press the Start button. Enter Scrapbook from the in-game Pause Menu. Enter the following code 3 times on the D-pad: Left, Up, A, X. Press this combination 3 times: Y, X. If done correctly you will hear a voice say, "Okay, let's play."

Exit out of the menu using the B Button. Select Exit Level and choose Yes to confirm your choice. Select Bonus from the Contents menu to view or enter the unlocked Bonus games.

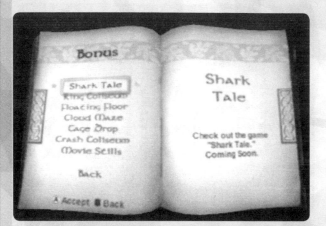

SONIC MEGA COLLECTION

BLUE SPHERE

Play Sonic 1 and Sonic 3D 20 times each.

THE COMIX ZONE

At the Manuals screen, press Z, Z, Z, Up, Up, Up, Down, Down, Down, L, R, Z.

FLICKY

Play Dr. Robotnik's Mean Bean Machine 20 times.

RISTAR

Play every game 20 times.

SONIC 2 AND KNUCKLES

Play Sonic 2 and Sonic Spinball 20 times each.

SONIC 3 AND KNUCKLES

Play Sonic 3 and Sonic and Knuckles 20 times each.

SONIC THE HEDGEHOG

LEVEL SELECT

At the Title screen, press Up, Down, Left, Right.

DEBUG MODE

At the Title screen, press Up, X, Down, X, Left, X, Right. Hold B, then hold Start until the level loads. Press A for Debug Mode.

SONIC THE HEDGEHOG 2

LEVEL SELECT

Select Sound Test from the Options menu and play the following sounds in order: 19, 65, 9, and 17. Hold X and press Start. At the Title screen, hold B and press Start.

DEBUG MODE

After enabling the Level Select code, use the Sound Test to play the following sounds in order: 1, 9, 9, 2, 1, 1, 2, 4. Select the desired level, then hold B + Start until the level loads.

SONIC THE HEDGEHOG 3

LEVEL SELECT

After the Sega logo fades, and as Sonic appears, press Up, Up, Down, Down, Up (x4). At the Title screen, press Up to access the Level Select.

DEBUG MODE

With the Level Select code enabled, hold B and press Start.

SONIC SPINBALL

LEVEL SELECT

At the Options menu, press B, Down, A, Down, X, Down, B, A, Up, B, X, Up, A, X, Up.

FLICKY

LEVEL SELECT

Start a game and hold Up + A + X + Start. When Round 1 appears, release the buttons.

RISTAR

Enter the following as passwords:

PASSWORD	EFFECT
ILOVEU	Level Select
MUSEUM	Bosses Only
SUPERB	Very Hard Difficulty
DOFEEL	Time Attack
MAGURO	Different Sounds
MIEMIE	Hidden Items
XXXXXX	Disable Codes

SPEED KINGS

Enter the following as your Handle:

COMPLETE DRIVING TEST
Enter .TEST9.

ALL MEETS WON
Enter .MEET6.

RESPECT POINTS
Enter .Resp ##.
Replace ## with the desired amount of respect.

MASTER CHEAT
Enter borkbork as a name.

SSX 3

Select Options from the Main Menu. Choose Cheat Codes from the Options menu, and enter the following codes to unlock each character. To access the characters, go to the Lodge, and select Rider Details. Then select Cheat Characters to find them.

BRODI
Enter zenmaster.

BUNNY SAN
Enter wheresyourtail.

CANHUCK
Enter greatwhitenorth.

CHURCHILL
Enter tankengine.

CUDMORE
Enter milkemdaisy.

EDDIE
Enter worm.

GUTLESS
Enter boneyardreject.

HIRO
Enter slicksuit.

JURGEN
Enter brokenleg.

LUTHER
Enter bronco.

MARTY
Enter back2future.

NORTH WEST LEGEND
Enter callhimgeorge.

SNOWBALLS
Enter betyouveneverseen.

STRETCH
Enter windmilldunk.

SVELTE LUTHER
Enter notsosvelte.

UNKNOWN RIDER
Enter finallymadeitin.

PEAK 1 CLOTHES
Enter shoppingspree.

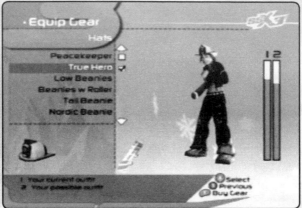

ALL BOARDS
Enter graphicdelight.

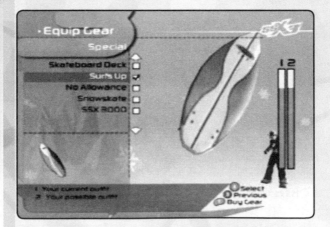

ALL PEAKS
Enter biggerthank7.

ALL ARTWORK
Enter naturalconcept.

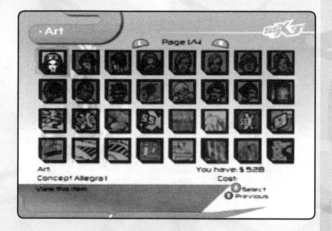

ALL VIDEOS
Enter myeyesaredim.

ALL PLAYLIST SONGS
Enter djsuperstar.

ALL TOYS

Enter nogluerequired.

ALL TRADING CARDS

Enter gotitgotitneedit.

ALL POSTERS

Enter postnobills.

TAK AND THE POWER OF JUJU

Pause the game and enter the following:

ALL EXTRAS AND CHEATS
Enter Left, Right, B, B, X, X, Left, Right.

100 FEATHERS
Enter B, Y, X, B, Y, X, B, Y.

ALL MOONSTONES
Enter Y, Y, B, B, X, X, Left, Right.

ALL PLANTS

Enter B, Y, X, Left, Up, Right, Down, Down.

ALL JUJU POWER-UPS

Enter Up, Right, Left, Down, Y, X, B, Down.

ALL YORBELS

Enter Up, Y, Left, B, Right, X, Down, Up.

TEENAGE MUTANT NINJA TURTLES

Select Password from the Options menu, and enter the following. Hold R or L at character select to select new costumes.

EFFECT	PASSWORD
Casey Jones	SRLMD
Master Splinter	LSLML
New Costume for Donatello	RRSLR
New Costume for Leonardo	RSLMD
New Costume for Michaelangelo	RLSLS
New Costume for Raphael	SLSMM
Something happened to Donatello	DRLDS
Something happened to Donatello	MLMLS
Something happened to Donatello	MLSDS
Something happened to Leonardo	LMLSD
Something happened to Leonardo	LDSMS

EFFECT	PASSWORD
Something happened to Leonardo	RSDMM
Something happened to Michelangelo	MRRML
Something happened to Michelangelo	MSRMM
Something happened to Michelangelo	RLMSM
Something happened to Michelangelo	RLDDR
Something happened to Raphael	RDSRL
Something happened to Raphael	SDRML
Something happened to Raphael	MSLLR
Something happened to Raphael	RSSSR
Something happened to Raphael	LSMMS
Something happened to Raphael	LSMMS
Something happened to Michaelangelo	MSSLD
Something happened to Leonardo	SSLDM
Change Hit Sound	DDDML
Playmates Database	LSDRM

TIGER WOODS PGA TOUR 2004

ALL GOLFERS AND COURSES
Enter THEKITCHENSINK.

ALL GOLFERS
Enter CANYOUPICKONE

ALL COURSES
Enter ALLTHETRACKS.

TARGET SHOOTOUT
Enter SHERWOODTARGET.

ACE ANDREWS
Enter ACEINTHEHOLE.

CEDRIC THE ENTERTAINER
Enter CEDDYBEAR.

DOMINIC "THE DON" DONATELLO
Enter DISCOKING.

DOWNTOWN BROWN
Enter DTBROWN.

EDWIN "POPS" MASTERSON
Enter EDDIE.

ERICA ICE
Enter ICYONE.

HAMISH "MULLIGAN" MEGREGOR
Enter DWILBY.

MOA "BIG MO" TA'A VATU
Enter ERUPTION.

SOLITA LOPEZ
Enter SHORTGAME.

SUNDAY TIGER
Enter 4REDSHIRTS.

TAKEHARU "TSUNAMI" MOTO
Enter EMERALDCHAMP.

VAL SUMMERS
Enter BEVERLYHILLS.

"YOSH" TANIGAWA
Enter THENEWLEFTY.

TIGER WOODS
PGA TOUR 2005

Select Passwords and enter the following:

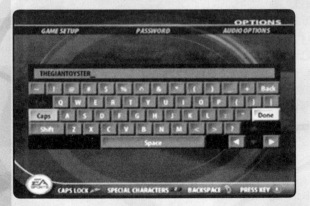

ALL GOLFERS AND COURSES
Enter THEGIANTOYSTER.

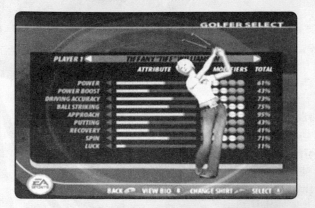

ALL COURSES
Enter THEWORLDISYOURS

THE CITY ROOFTOPS SKILL ZONE
Enter NIGHTGOLFER.

ADIDAS ITEMS
Enter 91treSTR

CALLAWAY ITEMS
Enter cgTR78qw

CLEVELAND ITEMS
Enter CL45etUB

MAXFLI ITEMS
Enter FDGH597i

NIKE ITEMS
Enter YJHk342B

ODYSSEY ITEMS
Enter kjnMR3qv

PING ITEMS
Enter R453DrTe

PRECEPT ITEMS
Enter BRi3498Z

TAG ITEMS
Enter cDsa2fgY

TOURSTAGE ITEMS
Enter TS345329

TIFFANY WILLIAMSON
Enter RICHGIRL

JEB "SHOOTER" MCGRAW
Enter SIXSHOOTER

HUNTER "STEELHEAD" ELMORE
Enter GREENCOLLAR

ALASTAIR" CAPTAIN" MCFADDEN
Enter NICESOCKS

BEV "BOOMER" BUOUCHIER
Enter THEBEEHIVE

ADRIANA "SUGAR" DULCE
Enter SOSWEET

APHRODITE PAPADAPOLUS
Enter TEMPTING

BILLY "BEAR" HIGHTOWER
Enter TOOTALL

KENDRA "SPIKE" LOVETTE
Enter ENGLISHPUNK

DION "DOUBLE D" DOUGLAS
Enter DDDOUGLAS

RAQUEL "ROCKY" ROGERS
Enter DOUBLER

BUNJIRO "BUD" TANAKA
Enter INTHEFAMILY

CEASAR "THE EMPEROR" ROSADO
Enter LANDOWNER

REGINALD WEATHERS
Enter REGGIE

THE HUSTLER
Enter ALTEREGO

SUNDAY TIGER WOODS
Enter NEWLEGEND

SEVE BALLESTEROS
Enter THEMAGICIAN

BEN HOGAN
Enter PUREGOLF

JACK NICKLAUS
Enter GOLDENBEAR.

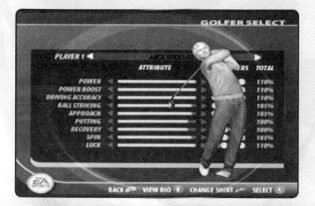

ARNOLD PALMER
Enter THEKING.

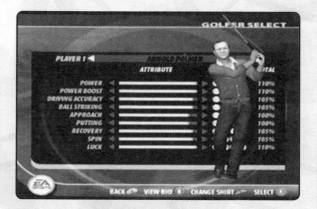

GARY PLAYER
Enter BLACKKNIGHT.

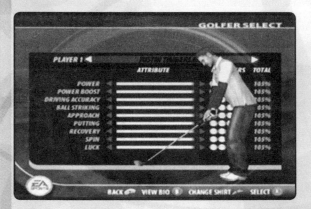

JUSTIN TIMBERLAKE
Enter THETENNESSEEKID.

TY THE TASMANIAN TIGER

SHOW HIDDEN OBJECTS
During gameplay, press L, R, L, R, Y, Y, X, B, B, X, Z, Z.

ALL ABILITIES
During gameplay, press L, R, L, R, Y, Y, B, B, Y, B.

TECHNORANGS
During gameplay, press L, R, L, R, Y, Y, Y, B, Y, B.

UNLIMITED LIFE
At the Main Menu, press L, R, L, R, Y, Y, Y, Y, X, X.

UNLOCK MOVIES
At the Main Menu, press L, R, L, R, Y, Y, A, A, Z, B, Z, B.

WHIRL TOUR

ALL CHARACTERS AND LEVELS
At the main menu, press Y, B, X, Y, Down, Right, Up, Left, L, L, Right, Right, Down, Up, R, X, Left, B, B, Down.

ALL LEVELS
At the main menu, press B, Y, X, B, L, X, R, L, X, R, B.

COMPLETE CURRENT OBJECTIVES
Pause the game and press X, X, B, X, X, Y, X, X, L, R.

YU-GI-OH! FALSEBOUND KINGDOM

GOLD COINS
On an empty piece of land, during a mission, press Up, Up, Down, Down, Left, Right, Left, Right, B, A.

Games

AGGRESSIVE INLINE 70

AMERICAN BASS CHALLENGE.. 70

AROUND THE WORLD IN 80 DAYS 70

ASTRO BOY: OMEGA FACTOR 71

BEYBLADE: ULTIMATE BLADER JAM 71

BRUCE LEE: RETURN OF THE LEGEND 73

BUBBLE BOBBLE OLD AND NEW.. 73

CAR BATTLER JOE 74

CORVETTE.. 75

CRASH BANDICOOT PURPLE: RIPTO'S RAMPAGE 75

CRASH NITRO KART 77

CRUIS'N VELOCITY.. 77

DAREDEVIL 79

DONKEY KONG COUNTRY 80

DONKEY KONG COUNTRY 2 80

E.T.: THE EXTRA-TERRESTRIAL 82

FAIRLY ODDPARENTS: BREAKIN' DA RULES 83

FINDING NEMO 83

GALIDOR: DEFENDERS OF THE OUTER DIMENSION............................ 83

GRADIUS GALAXIES 84

GREMLINS 84

GT ADVANCE 3: PRO CONCEPT RACING 84

ICE AGE 86

THE INCREDIBLE HULK 88

IRIDION II 88

JAZZ JACKRABBIT 89

KONAMI COLLECTOR'S SERIES: ARCADE ADVANCED........................ 90

THE LEGEND OF ZELDA (CLASSIC NES SERIES)................................ 90

MATCHBOX CROSS TOWN HEROES.. 91

MEGA MAN BATTLE NETWORK 3 92

MEGA MAN BATTLE NETWORK 4 93

MLB SLUGFEST 20-04 99

MUPPET PINBALL MAYHEM 99

MUPPETS: ON WITH THE SHOW! 100

PIRATES OF THE CARIBBEAN: THE CURSE OF THE BLACK PEARL............ 100

POKEMON FIRERED/POKEMON LEAFGREEN 100

POWER RANGERS: DINO THUNDER... 101

ROBOTECH: THE MACROSS SAGA 102

ROBOT WARS: EXTREME DESTRUCTION 102

ROCK 'N' ROLL RACING 102

SCOOBY-DOO 2: MONSTERS UNLEASHED 102

SEGA SMASH PACK 103

THE SIMPSONS: ROAD RAGE 103

SONIC BATTLE... 104

SPONGEBOB SQUAREPANTS: REVENGE OF THE FLYING DUTCHMAN 104

SPYRO ORANGE: THE CORTEX CONSPIRACY 105

SPYRO: SEASON OF FLAME... 106

STAR WARS EPISODE 2: THE NEW DROID ARMY 108

SUPER MONKEY BALL JR... 113

SUPER PUZZLE FIGHTER 2 TURBO... 114

TEENAGE MUTANT NINJA TURTLES 117

THUNDERBIRDS 117

TOP GUN: FIRESTORM ADVANCE 118

WARIO LAND 4 118

WILD THORNBERRYS:THE MOVIE 118

WORMS WORLD PARTY 119

X2: WOLVERINE'S REVENGE 119

YU-GI-OH! THE ETERNAL DUELIST SOUL 120

YU-GI-OH! RESHEF OF DESTRUCTION 120

YU-GI-OH! THE SACRED CARDS 122

YU-GI-OH! WORLDWIDE EDITION: STAIRWAY TO THE DESTINED DUEL ..122

AGGRESSIVE INLINE

ALL SKATERS

At the Title screen, press L, L, B, B, R, R, L, R.

LEVEL SELECT

At the Title screen, press Up, Down, Up, Down, Left, Right, B, R.

AMERICAN BASS CHALLENGE

ALL BASS

At the main menu, press Up, Up, Down, Left, Left, Right.

AROUND THE WORLD IN 80 DAYS

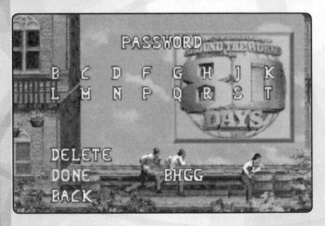

PASSWORDS

LEVEL	PASSWORD
Day 1 - London	BHGG
Day 3 - Paris	CLGG
Day 18 - Train	DCHJ
Day 20 - Turkey	FSHJ
Day 25 - India	GKMN
Day 25 - Wanted in India	HLSN

LEVEL	PASSWORD
Day 40 - China	JMBJ
Day 61 - San Francisco	KNQN
Day 61 - Train to New York	MQGG
Day 61 - Wild West	LPGG
Old Foe	NRGG
Ending	PSGG

ASTRO BOY: OMEGA FACTOR

SHARAKU
Let the ending credits run.

STAGE SELECT
Defeat the game. Pause the game to access the stage select.

BEYBLADE: ULTIMATE BLADER JAM

ALL BEYBLADES
At the title screen, press B, L, R, Down.

Name: Cyber Driger

○ Cyber Dranzer

○ Cyber Draciel

▷ ○ Cyber Driger

● Fox

○ Spider

DESTROY ENEMIES

Pause the game and press Up, Up, Right, Left, L.

FILL BIT BEAST ATTACK METER

Pause the game and press Right, Left, Right, Left.

BRUCE LEE: RETURN OF THE LEGEND

At the Select a Slot screen, hold L and enter the following codes:

TIME CHALLENGE
Press Up, Down, Up, R, Up, Down, Select.

HAI FENG IS INVINCIBLE
Press Down, Down, R, R, Up, Up, Select.

GALLERY
Press Down, Up, Down, R, R, Select, Left.

UNLIMITED AMMUNITION
Press R, Up, R, Up, R, Up, R.

SELECT BIG THUGS
Press Right, Left, Right, Left, Right, Left, Right.

SELECT TEXASES
Press Up, Down, Left, Right, Up, Down, Left.

SELECT JAMALS
Press Right (x7).

RANDOMIZE ALL ENEMIES
Press Up, Right, Down, R, R, Select, Left.

BRUCE '73 COSTUME
Press Right, Down, Down, R, R, Select, Left.

DRAGON COSTUME
Press Right, Up, Down, R, Up, Select, Left.

GOLD COSTUME
Press Right, Up, Up, R, R, Select, Left.

DIRECTOR'S CUT
Press Up, R, Select, R, Up, Select, Select.

BUBBLE BOBBLE OLD AND NEW

BUBBLE BOBBLE NEW: SUPER MODE
At the Bubble Bobble New title screen, press Right, R, Left, L, Select, R, Select, L.

BUBBLE BOBBLE OLD: ORIGINAL MODE

At the Bubble Bobble Old title screen, press L, R, L, R, L, R, Right, Select.

BUBBLE BOBBLE OLD: POWER-UP MODE

At the Bubble Bobble Old title screen, press Select, R, L, Left, Right, R, Select, Right.

BUBBLE BOBBLE OLD: SUPER MODE

At the Bubble Bobble Old title screen, press Left, R, Left, Select, Left, L, Left, Select.

CAR BATTLER JOE

JIM JOE ZERO CAR

In Battle League, enter TODOROKI as a password.

CORVETTE

SMALL CARS

During a game, hold L + R and press Up, Right, Down, Left, Right, Left, Right, Left.

CRASH BANDICOOT PURPLE: RIPTO'S RAMPAGE

100 WUMPA

At the Mode menu, press L + R, then enter CR4SH.

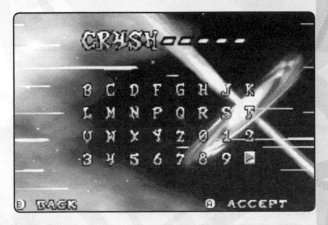

200 WUMPA

At the Mode menu, press L + R, then enter G3CK0.

500 WUMPA

At the Mode menu, press L + R, then enter C0FF33.

ORANGE GAME

At the Mode menu, press L + R, then enter L4MPP0ST.

GREEN PANTS

At the Mode menu, press L + R, then enter K1LL4Z.

GRENADES

At the Mode menu, press L + R, then enter STR4WB3RRY. Use the R Button to toss grenades.

SPYRO PARTY MINI-GAME

Turn on your Game Boy® Advance and hold L + R.

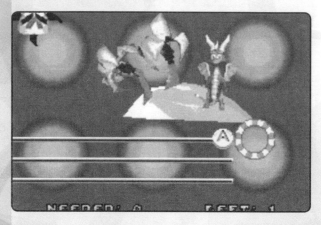

CREDITS

At the Mode menu, press L + R, then enter CR3D1TS.

CRASH NITRO KART

CRASH PARTY USA MINI-GAME

Hold L + R and turn on the game.

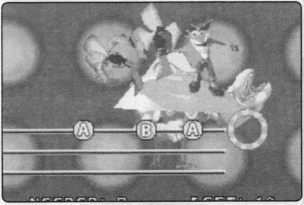

CRUIS'N VELOCITY

UNLOCK EVERYTHING

Enter RLCRHVGD as a password.

PASSWORD

RLCRHVGD

UP/DOWN SELECT CHARACTER
LEFT/RIGHT MOVE CURSOR
PRESS SELECT TO CLEAR

MIDWAY

A ACCEPT B BACK

CAR TYPE

SCORPION

SPEED: ★★★★★★
ACCEL: ★★★★★★
GRIP: ★★★★☆☆
TURBOS: ★★☆☆☆☆

◁ ● ▷

MIDWAY

A ACCEPT B BACK

CUP MODE

AMATEUR CUP
PRO CUP
VELOCITY CUP

MIDWAY

A ACCEPT B BACK

PASSWORDS

Enter the following as a password:

LEVEL	PASSWORD
Amateur Cup	HLDDRTSN

LEVEL	PASSWORD
Pro Cup	HLDDSNST
Velocity Cup	HLDDNRLN
Championship	HLDDHVGD

DAREDEVIL

UNLOCK EVERYTHING

Enter the password 41TK1S6ZNGV.

DONKEY KONG COUNTRY

50 LIVES
At the game select, highlight Erase. Then hold Select and press B, A, R, R, A, L.

DONKEY KONG COUNTRY 2

Select Cheats from the Options and enter the following:

LEVEL SELECT
Enter FREEDOM.

START WITH 15 LIVES
Enter HELPME.

START WITH 55 LIVES
Enter WEAKLING.

START WITH 10 BANANA COINS
Enter RICHMAN.

START WITH 50 BANANA COINS
Enter WELLRICH.

NO DK BARRELS
Enter WELLARD.

NO DK OR HALF-WAY BARRELS
Enter ROCKARD.

MUSIC TEST
Enter ONETIME.

CREDITS
Enter KREDITS.

E.T.: THE EXTRA-TERRESTRIAL

PASSWORDS

LEVEL	PASSWORD
2	Up, Up, A, Down, Down, B, L, R
3	Left, Up, Right, Down, L, A, R, B
4	A, Left, B, Right, L, Up, R, Down
5	L, R, R, L, A, Up, B, Left
6	L, Left, R, Right, A, A, B, A
7	B, R, B, L, A, Up, B, Up
8	Up, Up, A, Down, Down, Left, A, B
9	Right, B, B, Left, Up, R, R, L
10	Left, Left, A, L, Right, Right, B, R

FAIRLY ODDPARENTS: BREAKIN' DA RULES

CHEAT MODE

Enter X3YSV3!P as a password.

FINDING NEMO

LEVEL SELECT AND GALLERY

Enter the password M6HM.

PASSWORDS

LEVEL	PASSWORD
1	IH5I
2	HZ5I
3	ZZ5I
4	806I
5	7KPI
6	8JPI
7	3N6J
8	MP3K
9	L67K
10	45ZK
11	3NGH
12	4PHC

GALIDOR: DEFENDERS OF THE OUTER DIMENSION

INVINCIBILITY

At the title screen, hold R + L and press A, B, A, A, B.

GRADIUS GALAXIES

SLOWER

Pause the game and press Left, Right, Up, Down, Left, Left, Right, Start.

SELF-DESTRUCT

Pause the game and press Up, Up, Down, Down, Left, Right, Left, Right, B, A, Start.

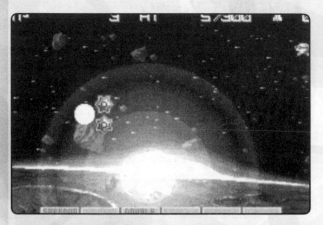

GREMLINS

LEVEL	PASSWORD	STRIPE TIME ATTACK
The Bank	GIZMO	CRUEL
The Police Station	BILLY	WATER
The Cinema	FUNNY	POWER
The Firehouse	TORCH	FLAME
The Final Encounter	GIFTS	MAGIC

GT ADVANCE 3: PRO CONCEPT RACING

ALL CARS

At the Title screen, hold L + B and press Left.

ALL TRACKS

At the Title screen, hold L + B and press Right.

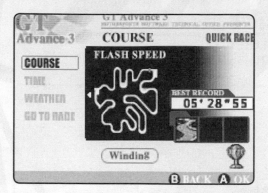

ALL TUNE UPS

At the Title screen, hold L + B and press Up.

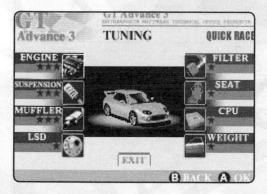

EXTRA MODES

At the Title screen, hold L + B and press Down.

ICE AGE

LEVEL SELECT

Enter NTTTTT as a password.

ART GALLERY

Enter MFKRPH as a password.

LEVEL PASSWORDS

LEVEL	PASSWORD
2	PBBQBB
3	QBCQBB
4	SBFQBB
5	DBKQBB
6	NBTQBB
7	PCTQBB
8	RFTQBB
9	CKTQBB
10	MTTQBB

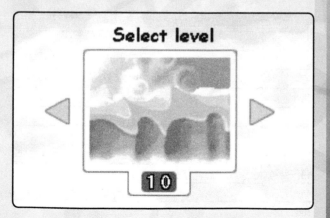

THE INCREDIBLE HULK

STAGE SKIP

Pause the game and press Down, Right, Down, Right, Left, Left, Left, Up.

IRIDION II

EASY PASSWORDS

LEVEL	PASSWORD
2	SBJS5
3	9CRT5
4	T3KG3
5	93PNV
6	95FN3
7	5MYCX
8	6C3L5
9	PW3NX
10	649QV
11	NFK2V
12	5DS2V
13	!GDV5
14	T7H8X
15	!9ROX
End	4RC8!

JUKEBOX

Enter CH4LL as a password.

JAZZ JACKRABBIT

500 CREDITS

Pause the game and press Right, Left, Right, Left, L, R, Up, Up, R, R, L, L.

1000 CREDITS

Pause the game and press Up, Down, Up, Down, Left, Right, L, R, L, R, R, L.

5000 CREDITS

Pause the game and press Up, Right, Down, Left, L, L, Right, Left, R, R, L, L.

KONAMI COLLECTOR'S SERIES: ARCADE ADVANCED

FROGGER: ADVANCED

At the Frogger title screen, press Up (x2), Down (x2), Left, Right, Left, Right, B, A, Start.

SCRAMBLE: ADVANCED

At the Scramble title screen, press Up (x2), Down (x2), Left, Right, Left, Right, B, A, Start.

TIME PILOT: RAPID FIRE AND NEW STAGE

At the Time Pilot title screen, press Up (x2), Down (x2), Left, Right, Left, Right, B, A, Start.

GYRUSS: ADVANCED

At the Gyruss title screen, press Up (x2), Down (x2), Left, Right, Left, Right, B, A, Start.

YIE-AR KUNG FU: ALL FIGHTERS IN MULTIPLAYER

At the Yie Ar Kung Fu title screen, press Up (x2), Down (x2), Left, Right, Left, Right, B, A, Start.

RUSH N' ATTACK: 2 EXTRA LIVES AND 2 NEW STAGES

At the Rush N' Attack title screen, press Up (x2), Down (x2), Left, Right, Left, Right, B, A, Start.

THE LEGEND OF ZELDA (CLASSIC NES SERIES)

SECOND QUEST

Enter ZELDA as a name.

MATCHBOX CROSS TOWN HEROES

Enter Password

C   B   C   T

B Cancel   OK A

PASSWORDS

LEVEL	PASSWORD
2	CBCT
3	QBKL
4	CBCL
5	QBVJ
6	QBDJ
End	QBVN

MEGA MAN BATTLE NETWORK 3

ERROR CODES

If you attempt to use a Program of a color your current Style does not support, you will get an Error and be unable to boot up Mega Man until the problem is fixed.

You can bypass these errors when you purchase the ModTools at Beach Street. When the Error number appears, press Select, and input the Code to counter. This only works if you have the proper Code for the specific Error. Error codes can be obtained by talking to the right people or reading BBSes, or looking at this list below.

ERROR	CODE
A3	LO13ZXME
B2	ALSK3W2R
B3	Y2UOMNCB
B5	BM2KWIRA
C2	UTIXM1LA
D2G	OI1UWMAN
E1	P2I3MSJL
F3	ITA2CRWQ
G2C	TIS1LAEJ
G2G	CVVDS2WR
H2	UTIW2SMF
S2C	TU1AW2LL
S2G	AX1RTDS3
S2S	F2AAFETG

MOD CODES

The ModTools can be used for more than just fixing program errors. With a properly-programmed Mega Man, hit Select when the "OK!" appears, then enter in a code from the list below for an added Program effect without taking up valuable real estate!

CODE	EFFECT
JIEU1AWT	HP+100
ZBKDEU1W	Block
UIEU2NGO	DashRun
PEOTIR2G	FlotShoe
SJH1UEKA	Humor
JDKGJ1U2	MegFldr1

COMPRESSION CODES

ModTools can be used in other ways. Highlight a Program in the list, then press and hold Select. Enter the right combination of buttons, and the Program will be compressed slightly, allowing you room for more Programs in the grid.

PROGRAM	COMPRESS CODE
BlckMind	Right,Left, Right,Down, R, Down
BrakChrg	B, A, Left, L, Up, B
BugStop	B, Down, Up, B, Down, B
Collect	B, Down, Right, R, Right,Right
DashRun	R, L, B, Down,Down,Down
Humor	Up, R, A, Left, Right,Right
MegFdlr2	A, R, Down,Down, Right,Left
OilBody	Up,Right, A, A, R, Up
SetMetl	B, R, Right,Right, L, L
SprArmor	Up,Right, Up, R, Up,Down

MEGA MAN BATTLE NETWORK 4

In order to get all chips, you must defeat the game multiple times. After the first defeat, you don't have all the Battle Chips and Navi Souls. Once you return to the main title screen, select Continue, and a new choice pops up. From here, you can return to your previous save point, or start a second version of the game.

From save point
▶Start game 2

Warning: It is *strongly* recommended that you collect *every* piece of Blue and Purple Mystery Data from the Cyberworld before you start the new game. Don't worry about clearing out the NetDealers, or human-world items; they will still be there.

You keep the neat stuff from the first game: Zenny, Chips, upgrades, Souls, and the Navi Customizer. Key Items, however, you have to get all over again. The viruses are more powerful in this game, but this is your chance to earn the higher-level Chips that were previously inaccessible.

Note: Don't forget to play the "Taiyohh!" sub-quest with Django and ShadeMan again. Not only does this cause ShadeMan SP to become a random-encounter enemy in Undernet 4 (allowing you to get his Chips), but it also nets you the **NebulaCd** to get those items once again blocked by skull-gates.

BATTLE CHIP CHALLENGE CODES

If you've been exploring everything, you should have acquired six NaviCodes. This chart lists them all, plus a special seventh code that gives you a shot at acquiring Chip #229, the HubStyle NaviChip!

NAME	NAVICODE
LAN	NG75-H5RF-R0MN-440N-2QX♣-X341
MAYL	8NT8-JZFL-3Q9D-7RPX-T♦CH-JX51
DEX	FD♠3-3JW1-PS♠V-♦01♦-♥6R♣-1J32
CHAU	93♣5-WXNH-9MWT-♠VX8-DY7M-88H0
KAI	M♠SP-3♥♦C-6KGQ-♥9FM-X0N♥-M♦P1
MARY	CX4♠-1GA9-5JKL-S♣GD-3L5B-90Z1
LAN	5♠4H-B81R-♠KKZ-P15X-ZS5B-♣XK0

NAVI SOULS

You only earn *two* of the three missing Navi Souls the second time through the game. The final Navi Soul eludes you until you defeat Duo again, and start a *third*, even harder version of the game!

In the third run-through, the game upgrades the Viruses once again, reshuffles the Mystery Data items, gives you a shot at obtaining Mr. Famous' **FamFldr**, and gives you the final Navi Soul to complete your set. Once you have six souls, you can enter Undernet 5.

UNDERNET 5

Be sure to have two Unlocker SubChips when you enter Undernet 5. The **NeoVari N** and **Snctuary S** Mega Chips are contained within purple Mystery Data packets.

To reach Bass, you must have an "S-ID." This means that once you complete the Standard Chips portion of your data Library, the door will open. Once Bass is defeated, he retreats to the darkest portion of the Undernet: Black Earth. But not before he leaves behind a Giga Chip for you: **Bass X** in *Red Sun*, **BassAnly X** in *Blue Moon*. Before you can follow Bass into the Black Earth, you must collect five dark Mega Chips from the denizens of the Undernet. Four of them are in Undernet 5. Jack Out of the net, then return; otherwise the three guardians of the Chips do not appear.

BUGCHARG/BUGCURSE

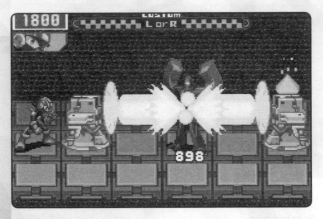

When you face DarkMan SP in Undernet 4, or LaserMan SP in Undernet 5, there's a green Mystery Data packet waiting in the back column. These packets contain the version-specific Giga Chips **BugCharg** (in *Red Sun*), or **BugCurse** (in *Blue Moon*).

ANUBIS

Three of the dark Chips you need are within Undernet 5, held by HeelNavis. The HeelNavi at the bottom of the area by the locked Mystery Data has the **Anubis** Mega Chip.

BLAKWING

> But thanks to you,
> Bass was defeated
> and I was freed!

Make your way to the back of the area where the **Snctuary** Chip sits in a purple Mystery Data. The second HeelNavi guardian is there, and he's got the **BlakWing**.

MURAMASA

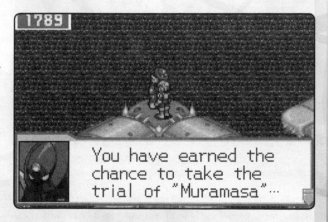

> You have earned the
> chance to take the
> trial of "Muramasa"…

The last of the three guardian HeelNavis is on the other side of the area, and he has the cursed blade **Muramasa**.

ELEMDARK

ElemDark is obtained by hunting down and defeating the ElemperorEX, an elusive Virus found only within Undernet 6.

BLACK EARTH 1/BLACK EARTH 2

> This door opens only to those without "V" who know fragments.

The gate at the end of Black Earth 1 opens after you collect the 12 version-specific normal and SP Navi Chips. These are the Navis whose souls resonate within MegaMan. Remember, you must defeat the SP Navis with an "S" Busting Level in order to acquire their SP Navi Chip!

In order to get the final Giga Chip you need to complete your Library (either **BlakAura** or **DeltaRay**), you must hunt down Bass SP within Black Earth 2. Jack Out, then return to set Bass SP as a random-encounter enemy. Defeat him, and the final Giga Chip is yours.

MLB SLUGFEST 20-04

CHEATS

Enter the following codes at the Matchup screen using the B, A, and R buttons. For example, for All Fielders Run (132 Up), press B once, A three times, and R twice, then press Up.

EFFECT	CODE
1920 Mode	242 Up
All Fielders Run	132 Up
Backwards Fielders	444 Right
Fireworks	141 Right
Ghost Fielders	313 Down
Nuke Ball	343 Up
Skull Ball	323 Left

MUPPET PINBALL MAYHEM

ANIMAL MACHINE

At the Options screen, select Credits. Then press Left, Right, Right, Up, R, Down, Down, L.

MUPPETS: ON WITH THE SHOW!

ALL MINI-GAMES
Enter the password J09J4.

MEDIUM DIFFICULTY
Enter the password G07n0.

HARD DIFFICULTY
Enter the password H08L2.

PIRATES OF THE CARIBBEAN: THE CURSE OF THE BLACK PEARL

UNLIMITED LIVES
Enter 1MM0RT4L as a password.

UNLIMITED CANNONBALLS AND BULLETS
Enter BVLL1TZ as a password.

START WITH TRIPLE CANNONS, SABER, AND PISTOL
Enter G00D13S as a password.

SOLDIERS AND PIRATES BECOME SHEEP
Enter SH33P as a password.

SMARTER AI
Enter G3N1VS as a password.

CREDITS
Enter CR3D1TS as a password.

BABY
Enter L1TTLVN as a password.

POKÉMON FIRERED/ POKÉMON LEAFGREEN

MYSTERY GIFT
At a Pokemon Center, find the clipboard by the shop and enter Link Together With All.

POWER RANGERS: DINO THUNDER

PASSWORDS

LEVEL	EASY	NORMAL	HARD
Blue Ranger 1	QVB	QVN	LWB
Blue Ranger 2	L60	L66	Q7J
Blue Ranger 3	28Z	Z88	69G
Blue Ranger 4	9XJ	9XQ	5YJ
Megazord 1	LZC	LZP	Q!Y
Megazord 2	G0Y	G03	B1Y
Megazord 3	L21	L27	Q3K
Megazord 4	24!		65H
Megazord 5	0ZH	0ZT	X!H
Megazord 6	50K	50R	91!
Megazord 7	121	127	Y31
Puzzle 1	BGW	BG5	GHC
Puzzle 2	L0Y	L03	Q1F
Puzzle 3	G4K	G4R	B5K
Puzzle 4	4ZH	4ZT	8!1
Red Ranger 1	GBV	GB4	BCV
Red Ranger 2	QXX	QX2	LYX
Red Ranger 3	XVZ	XV8	0WG
Red Ranger 4	YX0	YX6	1YJ
Red Ranger 5	160	166	Y70
Yellow Ranger 1	BXB	BXN	GYX
Yellow Ranger 2	G60	G66	B7Q
Yellow Ranger 3	G8J	G8Q	B9J
Yellow Ranger 4	8VG	8VS	4WG

VIEW CREDITS

Enter THQ as a password.

ROBOTECH: THE MACROSS SAGA

ALL CHARACTERS
At the title screen, press Down (x5), R, R.

MAX UPGRADES
At the title screen, press Up, Right, Down, Left, R, L (x3).

UNLIMITED LIVES
At the title screen, press Right (x3), Up, Up, L, L.

LEVEL SELECT
At the title screen, press Up, Down, Up, Down, L, R, L, R.

ROBOT WARS: EXTREME DESTRUCTION

INVINCIBILITY
Create a robot with the name HARD CASE.

ALL PARTS
Create a robot with the name SCRAP METAL.

ALL ARENAS
Create a robot with the name GLADIATOR.

ROCK 'N' ROLL RACING

OLAF
At the driver select, highlight Tarquinn, hold L + R + Select and press Right.

INFERNO LEVEL IN VERSUS
At the planet select, highlight NHO, hold L + R + Select and press Right.

SCOOBY-DOO 2: MONSTERS UNLEASHED

ALTERNATE ENDING
After you beat the game, enter SD2.

SEGA SMASH PACK

ECCO THE DOLPHIN

Pause the game with Ecco facing the screen and press Right, B, R, B, R, Down, R, Up. This unlocks Stage Select, Sound Select, and Unlimited Lives.

GOLDEN AXE

Select arcade mode and hold Down/Left + B and press Start at the Character Select screen. This unlocks Level Select.

GOLDEN AXE

Select arcade mode and hold Down/Left + A + R. Release the buttons and press Start to gain Nine Continues.

SONIC SPINBALL

At the Options screen, press A, Down, B, Down, R, Down, A, B, Up, A, R, Up, B, R, Up. This unlocks Level Select. The following commands will start you at that level.

LEVEL	COMMAND
2 Lava Powerhouse	Hold A and press START
3 The Machine	Hold B and press START
4 Showdown	Hold R and press START

SONIC SPINBALL

At the Options screen, press A, Up, R, Up, L, Up, A, R, Down, A, L, Down, R, L, Down. This unlocks the game's Credits.

THE SIMPSONS: ROAD RAGE

Enter the following codes as passwords.

ALL CARS, LEVELS AND BONUSES

Enter Maggie, Willy, Bart, Chief Wiggum, Apu, Moe, Krusty, Barney.

ALL CHARACTERS

Enter Bart, Bart, Lisa, Lisa, Marge, Marge, Barney, Barney.

SONIC BATTLE

COMBO CARDS

During Emerl's Episode, enter the Sonic Team building at the south end of Central City. Enter one of the case-sensitive passwords below to unlock a character's combo card. You'll find their card under GRND POWER in the Edit Skills menu.

PASSWORD	CHARACTER
alogK	Amy
EkiTa	Chaos
Zahan	Cream
TSueT	E-102
yU3Da	Knuckles
AhnVo	Rouge
Armla	Shadow
75619	Sonic
OtrOl	Tails

SPONGEBOB SQUAREPANTS: REVENGE OF THE FLYING DUTCHMAN

DEBUG MODE

Enter the password D3BVG-M0D3.

SPYRO ORANGE: THE CORTEX CONSPIRACY

100 GEMS

At the Mode menu, press L + R, then enter V1S10NS.

ORANGE GAME

At the Mode menu, press L + R, then enter SP4RX.

PURPLE GAME

At the Mode menu, press L + R, then enter PORT4L.

ORANGE SPYRO

At the Mode menu, press L + R, then enter SPYR0.

SHEEP MODE

At the Mode menu, press L + R, then enter SH33P.

SHEEP FLAME MODE

At the Mode menu, press L + R, then enter B41S0KV.

CRASH PARTY USA MINI-GAME
Start up your Game Boy Advance and hold L + R.

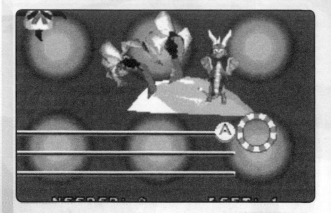

SPYRO: SEASON OF FLAME

BLUE SPYRO
At the Title screen, press Up, Up, Up, Up, Down, Left, Right, Down, B.

ALL PORTALS
At the Title screen, press Up, Left, Up, Right, Up, Down, Up, Down, B.

Celestial Plains

ALL WORLDS IN ATLAS

At the Title screen, press Left, Right, Up, Up, Right, Left, Right, Up, B.

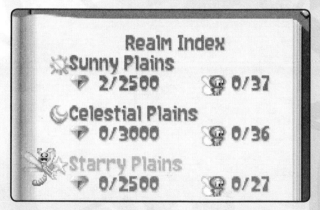

ATLAS WARPING

At the Title screen, press Down, Up, Left, Left, Up, Left, Left, Right, B.

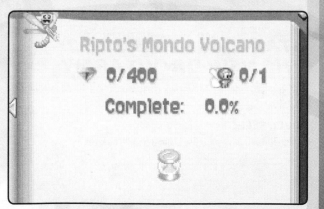

INFINITE LIVES

At the Title screen, press Left, Right, Left, Right (x3), Up, Down, B.

INFINITE SHIELD FOR AGENT 9

At the Title screen, press Left, Down, Up, Right, Left, Up, Up, Left, B.

INFINITE AMMO

At the Title screen, press Right, Left, Up, Down, Right, Down, Up, Right, B.

NEVER DROWN

At the Title screen, press Down, Up, Right, Left, Right, Up, Right, Left, B.

ALL BREATH TYPES

At the Title screen, press Right, Down, Up, Right, Left, Up, Right, Down, B.

SUPER CHARGE

At the Title screen, press Left, Left, Down, Up, Up, Right, Left, Left, B.

DRAGON DRAUGHTS MINI-GAME

At the Title screen, press Right, Up, Down, Down, Down, Right, Up, Down, B.

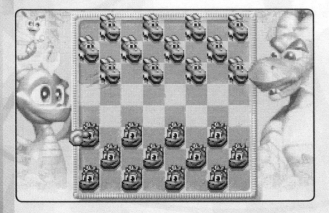

STAR WARS EPISODE 2: THE NEW DROID ARMY

After correctly entering the following passwords, you should receive an Invalid Password message.

LEVEL SELECT

Enter 2D4 as a password. Use L and R to select a level.

200 HEALTH AND 200 FORCE
Enter 8!T as a password.

ALL FORCE ABILITIES
Enter FRC as a password.

LUKE SKYWALKER
Enter SKY as a password.

OVERHEAD MAP
Enter CQL as a password.

CHANGE CONTROLS
Enter BTW as a password.

DISABLE SHADOW
Enter !B4 as a password.

BLACK SHADOWS
Enter SK8 as a password.

REDUCE RESOLUTION

Enter GFX as a password.

TOGGLE LANGUAGE OPTION

Enter LNG as a password. Select Language from the Options screen.

PASSWORDS

After correctly entering the following passwords, you should receive a password accepted message.

LEVEL	PASSWORD
Droids at Speeder	D31
Mos Espa	QK1
Xelric Draw	BKT
Womp Rat Cave	FKW
Xelric Draw	C3P
Xelric Draw	CYD
Mos Espa	AK?
Hutt's Assassins	A3W
Mos Espa	AY4
Dune Sea	KK4
Moisture Farms	M34
Moisture Farms	MYW
Jundland Wastes	TKP
Jundland Wastes	T3H
Jundland Wastes	TYQ
Jabba's Dungeon	J38
Jabba's Dungeon	JY1
Jabba's Dungeon	J?T
Jabba's Dungeon	J7J
High City	7KQ
High City	73D
High City (Interior)	7YP
High City (Interior)	7?W
Underlevels	!3C
Underlevels	!YL
Bentho's Nightclub	H3D
Core Bay	6K7
Core Bay	63L
Jedi Temple	532
Jedi Archives	4KX
Jedi Archives	438
Droid Factory Outskirts	XK1
Production Facility 1	23X
Production Facility 1	2Y7
Production Facility 2	3K2

LEVEL	PASSWORD
Production Facility 2	334
Cortosis Processing Plant	WKP
Dual Duel!	W3H
Dual Duel!	WYQ
Droid Factory Core	?KH
Droid Factory Core	?3P
Duel with Vandalor	8K7
Race the Bombs	831
Ending	Y3W

SUPER MONKEY BALL Jr.

ENABLE ALL

At the title screen, press Down, Down, Up, Up, Left, Right, Left, Right, B, A.

BLOCKY MODE

At the title screen, press Left, Left, Right, Right, Down, Down, A.

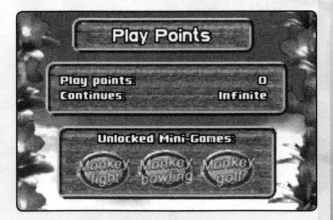

NICE TRY
At the title screen, press Up, Up, Down, Down, Left, Right, Left, Right, B, A.

SUPER PUZZLE FIGHTER 2 TURBO

AKUMA PLAYER 1
Highlight Morrigan, hold Select, press Down (3x), Left (3x), A.

AKUMA PLAYER 2
Highlight Felicia, hold Select, press Down (3x), Right (3x), A.

ANITA PLAYER 1

Highlight Morrigan, hold Select, move to Donovan and press A.

ANITA PLAYER 2

Highlight Felicia, hold Select, move to Donovan and press A.

DAN PLAYER 1

Highlight Morrigan, hold Select, press Left (3x), Down (3x), A.

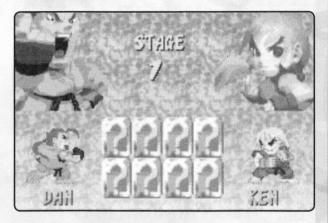

DAN PLAYER 2

Highlight Felicia, hold Select, press Right (3x), Down (3x), A

DEVILOT

Highlight Morrigan, hold Select, press Left (3x), Down (3x), A as the timer hits 10.

HSIEN-KO'S PAPER TALISMAN PLAYER 1

Highlight Morrigan, hold Select, move to Hsien-Ko and press A.

HSIEN-KO'S PAPER TALISMAN PLAYER 2

Highlight Felicia, hold Select, move to Hsien-Ko and press A.

TEENAGE MUTANT NINJA TURTLES

VERY HARD DIFFICULTY

At the title screen, press Up, Up, Down, Down, Left, Right, Left, Right, B, A.

THUNDERBIRDS

PASSWORDS

PASSWORD	MISSION
H3D	Flight mission 1
3M7	Flight mission 3
D8D	Flight mission 4
48D	Flight mission 5
T25	Flight mission 5
B9T	Flight mission 6
BCD	Mission 1
2DF	Mission 2
T89	Mission 3
MB2	Mission 4
F8H	Mission 5
4TH	Mission 6
6DC	Mission 7
F24	Mission 8
76H	Final mission
734	Credits

TOP GUN: FIRESTORM ADVANCE

PASSWORDS

LEVEL	PASSWORD
2	Jet, Missile, Jet, Jet
3	Top View Car, Side View Car, Tank, Missile
4	Boat, Missile, Boat, Missile
5	Boat, Top View Car, Jet, Missile Man
6	AA Gun, Top View Car, Boat, Top View Car
7	Side View Car, Side View Car, Missile, Jet
8	Paratrooper, AA Gun, Paratrooper, AA Gun
9	Missile Man, AA Gun, Jet, Tank
10	Missile, Missile, Top View Car, Paratrooper
11	Top View Car, AA Gun, AA Gun, Boat
12	Missile, Side View Car, Tank, Paratrooper

WARIO LAND 4

KARAOKE MODE

At the Sound Room, highlight Exit and hold Select + Start, + Up +
L + R.

WILD THORNBERRYS: THE MOVIE

LEVEL SELECT

Enter HB5F as a password.

WORMS WORLD PARTY

ALL WEAPONS

During gameplay, open the Weapon Select menu. Highlight Skip Go and press A. Return to the Weapon Select screen, hold L + Down + B, and press SELECT (x4).

X2: WOLVERINE'S REVENGE

Enter the following codes at the Slot select:

100 LIVES

Hold L, press Right (7x).

ALL POWER-UPS

Hold L, press Right, Left, Right, Left, Right, Left, Right.

INFINITE DOUBLE JUMP

Hold L, press Select, Left, Up, Down, Down, Up, Down.

INVINCIBILITY

Hold L, press Down, Up, Down, Down, Up, Down, Select.

REGENERATE WITH CLAWS EXTENDED

Hold L, press Right, Up, Down, Right, Left, Select, Select.

YU-GI-OH! THE ETERNAL DUELIST SOUL

See passwords in following section.

YU-GI-OH! RESHEF OF DESTRUCTION

Access the Password Terminal inside the card shop. For 1000 Domino, you can enter one of the following passwords in the next section.

You can enter a password for 1000 Domino.

38247752

7	8	9
4	5	6
1	2	3
0		OK

Dark-Eyes Illusionist

Dark-Eyes

Type	Magician
Summon	Dreams
Cost	10

A pathetic being with an ATK and DEF rating of 0 for both.

YU-GI-OH! THE SACRED CARDS

See passwords in following section.

YU-GI-OH! WORLDWIDE EDITION: STAIRWAY TO THE DESTINED DUEL

The following passwords work for The Eternal Duelist Soul, Reshef of Destruction, The Sacred Cards, and Worldwide Edition: Stairway to the Destined Duel.

PASSWORDS

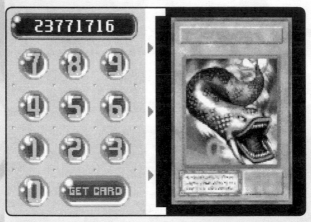

CARD	PASSWORD
7 Colored Fish	23771716
7 Completed	86198326
Acid Crawler	77568553
Acid Trap Hole	41356845
Air Eater	08353769
Air Marmot of Nefariousness	75889523
Akakieisu	38035986
Akihiron	36904469
Alligator's Sword	64428736
Alligator's Sword Dragon	03366982
Alpha The Magnet Warrior	99785935
Amazon of the Seas	17968114
Ameba	95174353
Amphibious Bugroth	40173854
Ancient Brain	42431843
Ancient Elf	93221206
Ancient Jar	81492226
Ancient Lizard Warrior	43230671
Ancient One of the Deep Forest	14015067
Ancient Telescope	17092736
Ancient Tool	49587396
Ansatsu	48365709
Anthrosaurus	89904598
Anti Raigeki	42364257
Anti-Magic Fragrance	58921041
Appropriate	48539234
Aqua Chorus	95132338
Aqua Dragon	86164529
Aqua Madoor	85639257
Arlownay	14708569
Arma Knight	36151751
Armaill	53153481
Armed Ninja	09076207
Armored Glass	36868108
Armored Lizard	15480588
Armored Rat	16246527

CARD	PASSWORD
Armored Starfish	17535588
Armored Zombie	20277860
Axe of Despair	40619825
Axe Raider	48305365
Baby Dragon	88819587
Backup Soldier	36280194
Banisher of the Light	61528025
Barox	06840573
Barrel Dragon	81480460
Barrel Lily	67841515
Barrel Rock	10476868
Basic Insect	89091579
Battle Ox	05053103
Battle Steer	18246479
Battle Warrior	55550921
Bean Soldier	84990171
Beast Fangs	46009906
Beastking of the Swamps	99426834
Beautiful Headhuntress	16899564
Beaver Warrior	32452818
Behegon	94022093
Bell of Destruction	83555666
Beta The Magnet Warrior	39256679
Bickuribox	25655502
Big Eye	16768387
Big Insect	53606874
Big Shield Gardna	65240384
Binding Chain	08058240
Bio Plant	07670542
Black Dragon Jungle King	89832901
Black Illusion Ritual	41426869
Black Pendant	65169794
Blackland Fire Dragon	87564352
Bladefly	28470714
Blast Juggler	70138455
Blast Sphere	26302522

CARD	PASSWORD
Block Attack	25880422
Blue Medicine	20871001
Blue-Eyed Silver Zombie	35282433
Blue-Eyes Toon Dragon	53183600
Blue-Eyes White Dragon	89631139
Blue-Eyes White Dragon	80906030
Blue-Winged Crown	41396436
Boar Soldier	21340051
Bolt Escargot	12146024
Book of Secret Arts	91595718
Bottom Dweller	81386177
Bracchio-Raidus	16507828
Breath of Light	20101223
Bright Castle	82878489
Burglar	06297941
Burning Spear	18937875
Buster Blader	78193831
Call of the Dark	78637313
Call of the Grave	16970158
Call Of The Haunted	97077563
Candle of Fate	47695416
Cannon Soldier	11384280
Castle of Dark Illusions	00062121
Castle Walls	44209392
Catapult Turtle	95727991
Ceasefire	36468556
Celtic Guardian	91152256
Ceremonial Bell	20228463
Chain Destruction	01248895
Chain Energy	79323590
Change of Heart	04031928
Charubin the Fire Knight	37421579
Chorus of Sanctuary	81380218
Claw Reacher	41218256
Clown Zombie	92667214
Cockroach Knight	33413638

CARD	PASSWORD
Confiscation	17375316
Crass Clown	93889755
Crawling Dragon	67494157
Crawling Dragon #2	38289717
Crazy Fish	53713014
Crimson Sunbird	46696593
Crow Goblin	77998771
Crush Card	57728570
Curse of Dragon	28279543
Curse of Fiend	12470447
Curtain of the Dark Ones	22026707
Cyber Commander	06400512
Cyber Falcon	30655537
Cyber Jar	34124316
Cyber Saurus	89112729
Cyber Shield	63224564
Cyber Soldier	44865098
Cyber-Stein	69015963
Cyber-Tech Alligator	48766543
Dancing Elf	59983499
Dark Artist	72520073
Dark Assailant	41949033
Dark Chimera	32344688
Dark Elf	21417692
Dark Energy	04614116
Dark Gray	09159938
Dark Hole	53129443
D. Human	81057959
Dark King of the Abyss	53375573
Dark Magician	46986414
Dark Rabbit	99261403
Dark Sage	92377303
Dark Shade	40196604
Dark Witch	35565537
Dark Zebra	59784896
Dark-Eyes Illusionist	38247752

CARD	PASSWORD
Darkfire Dragon	17881964
Darkfire Soldier #1	05388481
Darkfire Soldier #2	78861134
Darkness Approaches	80168720
Dark-Piercing Light	45895206
Darkworld Thorns	43500484
Deepsea Shark	28593363
Delinquent Duo	44763025
De-Spell	19159413
Destroyer Golem	73481154
Dice Armadillo	69893315
Dimensional Warrior	37043180
Disk Magician	76446915
Dissolverock	40826495
DNA Surgery	74701381
Dokuroizo the Grim Reaper	25882881
Doma The Angel of Silence	16972957
Doron	00756652
Dorover	24194033
Dragon Capture Jar	50045299
Dragon Piper	55763552
Dragon Seeker	28563545
Dragon Treasure	01435851
Dragon Zombie	66672569
Dragoness the Wicked Knight	70681994
Dream Clown	13215230
Driving Snow	00473469
Drooling Lizard	16353197
Dryad	84916669
Dunames Dark Witch	12493482
Dungeon Worm	51228280
Dust Tornado	60082869
Earthshaker	60866277
Eatgaboon	42578427
Eldeen	06367785
Electric Lizard	55875323

CARD	PASSWORD
Electric Snake	11324436
Electro-Whip	37820550
Elegant Egotist	90219263
Elf's Light	39897277
Empress Judge	15237615
Enchanted Javelin	96355986
Enchanting Mermaid	75376965
Eradicating Aerosol	94716515
Eternal Draught	56606928
Eternal Rest	95051344
Exchange	05556668
Exile of the Wicked	26725158
Exodia the Forbidden One	33396948
Eyearmor	64511793
Fairy Dragon	20315854
Fairy's Hand Mirror	17653779
Fairywitch	37160778
Faith Bird	75582395
Fake Trap	03027001
Feral Imp	41392891
Fiend Kraken	77456781
Fiend Reflection #1	68870276
Fiend Reflection #2	02863439
Fiend Sword	22855882
Fiend's Hand	52800428
Final Flame	73134081
Fire Kraken	46534755
Fire Reaper	53581214
Firegrass	53293545
Fireyarou	71407486
Fissure	66788016
Flame Cerebrus	60862676
Flame Champion	42599677
Flame Ghost	58528964
Flame Manipulator	34460851
Flame Swordsman	45231177

CARD	PASSWORD
Flame Viper	02830619
Flash Assailant	96890582
Flower Wolf	95952802
Flying Kamakiri #1	84834865
Flying Kamakiri #2	03134241
Follow Wind	98252586
Forced Requisition	74923978
Forest	87430998
Frenzied Panda	98818516
Fusion Sage	26902560
Fusionist	01641882
Gaia Power	56594520
Gaia the Dragon Champion	66889139
Gaia The Fierce Knight	06368038
Gale Dogra	16229315
Gamma the Magnet Warrior	11549357
Ganigumo	34536276
Garma Sword	90844184
Garma Sword Oath	78577570
Garnecia Elefantis	49888191
Garoozis	14977074
Garvas	69780745
Gatekeeper	19737320
Gazelle the King of Mythical Beasts	05818798
Gemini Elf	69140098
Genin	49370026
Germ Infection	24668830
Ghoul with an Appetite	95265975
Giant Flea	41762634
Giant Germ	95178994
Giant Mech-Soldier	72299832
Giant Rat	97017120
Giant Red Seasnake	58831685
Giant Scorpion of the Tundra	41403766
Giant Soldier of Stone	13039848
Giant Trunade	42703248

CARD	PASSWORD
Giant Turtle Who Feeds on Flames	96981563
Gift of The Mystical Elf	98299011
Giganto	33621868
Giga-tech Wolf	08471389
Giltia the D. Knight	51828629
Goblin Fan	04149689
Goblin's Secret Remedy	11868825
Goddess of Whim	67959180
Goddess with the Third Eye	53493204
Gokibore	15367030
Graceful Charity	79571449
Graceful Dice	74137509
Grappler	02906250
Gravedigger Ghoul	82542267
Gravekeeper's Servant	16762927
Graverobber	61705417
Graveyard and the Hand of Invitation	27094595
Great Bill	55691901
Great Mammoth of Goldfine	54622031
Great White	13429800
Green Phantom King	22910685
Greenkappa	61831093
Griffore	53829412
Griggle	95744531
Ground Attacker Bugroth	58314394
Gruesome Goo	65623423
Gryphon Wing	55608151
Guardian of the Labyrinth	89272878
Guardian of the Sea	85448931
Guardian of the Throne Room	47879985
Gust	73079365
Gust Fan	55321970
Gyakutenno Megami	31122090
Hane-Hane	07089711
Haniwa	84285623
Happy Lover	99030164

CARD	PASSWORD
Hard Armor	20060230
Harpie Lady	76812113
Harpie Lady Sisters	12206212
Harpie's Brother	30532390
Harpie's Feather Duster	18144506
Harpie's Pet Dragon	52040216
Heavy Storm	19613556
Hercules Beetle	52584282
Hero of the East	89987208
Hibikime	64501875
High Tide Gyojin	54579801
Hinotama	46130346
Hinotama Soul	96851799
Hiro's Shadow Scout	81863068
Hitodenchak	46718686
Hitotsu-Me Giant	76184692
Holograh	10859908
Horn Imp	69669405
Horn of Heaven	98069388
Horn of Light	38552107
Horn of the Unicorn	64047146
Hoshiningen	67629977
Hourglass of Courage	43530283
Hourglass of Life	08783685
House of Adhesive Tape	15083728
Hunter Spider	80141480
Hyo	38982356
Hyosube	02118022
Hyozanryu	62397231
Ice Water	20848593
Ill Witch	81686058
Illusionist Faceless Mage	28546905
Imperial Order	61740673
Insect Armor with Laser Cannon	03492538
Insect Queen	91512835
Insect Soldiers of the Sky	07019529

CARD	PASSWORD
Inspection	16227556
Invader from Another Dimension	28450915
Invader of the Throne	03056267
Invigoration	98374133
Jellyfish	14851496
Jigen Bakudan	90020065
Jinzo	77585513
Jinzo #7	32809211
Jirai Gumo	94773007
Judge Man	30113682
Just Desserts	24068492
Kagemusha of the Blue Flame	15401633
Kageningen	80600490
Kairyu-Shin	76634149
Kaiser Dragon	94566432
Kamakiriman	68928540
Kaminari Attack	09653271
Kaminarikozou	15510988
Kamionwizard	41544074
Kanikabuto	84103702
Karate Man	23289281
Karbonala Warrior	54541900
Kattapillar	81179446
Key Mace #2	20541432
Killer Needle	88979991
King Fog	84686841
King of Yamimakai	69455834
Kiseitai	04266839
Kojikocy	01184620
Kotodama	19406822
Koumori Dragon	67724379
Krokodilus	76512652
Kumootoko	56283725
Kunai with Chain	37390589
Kurama	85705804
Kuriboh	40640057

CARD	PASSWORD
Kwagar Hercules	95144193
La Jinn the Mystical Genie of the Lamp	97590747
Labyrinth Tank	99551425
Lady of Faith	17358176
LaLa Li-oon	09430387
Larvae	94675535
Laser Cannon Armor	77007920
Last Day of Witch	90330453
Last Will	85602018
Laughing Flower	42591472
Launcher Spider	87322377
Lava Battleguard	20394040
Left Arm of the Forbidden One	07902349
Left Leg of the Forbidden One	44519536
Legendary Sword	61854111
Leghul	12472242
Leogun	10538007
Lesser Dragon	55444629
Light of Intervention	62867251
Lightforce Sword	49587034
Liquid Beast	93108297
Little Chimera	68658728
Little D	42625254
Lord of D	17985575
Lord of the Lamp	99510761
Lord of Zemia	81618817
Luminous Spark	81777047
Lunar Queen Elzaim	62210247
Mabarrel	98795934
Machine Conversion Factory	25769732
Machine King	46700124
Magic Jammer	77414722
Magic Thorn	53119267
Magical Ghost	46474915
Magical Hats	81210420
Magical Labyrinth	64389297

CARD	PASSWORD
Magic-Arm Shield	96008713
Magician of Faith	31560081
Maha Vailo	93013676
Maiden of the Moonlight	79629370
Major Riot	09074847
Malevolent Nuzzler	99597615
Mammoth Graveyard	40374923
Man Eater	93553943
Man-Eater Bug	54652250
Man-Eating Black Shark	80727036
Man-Eating Plant	49127943
Man-Eating Treasure Chest	13723605
Manga Ryu-Ran	38369349
Marine Beast	29929832
Masaki the Legendary Swordsman	44287299
Mask of Darkness	28933734
Masked Sorcerer	10189126
Master & Expert	75499502
Mavelus	59036972
Mechanical Snail	34442949
Mechanical Spider	45688586
Mechanicalchaser	07359741
Meda Bat	76211194
Mega Thunderball	21817254
Megamorph	22046459
Megazowler	75390004
Meotoko	53832650
Mesmeric Control	48642904
Messenger of Peace	44656491
Metal Detector	75646520
Metal Dragon	09293977
Metal Fish	55998462
Metal Guardian	68339286
Metalmorph	68540058
Metalzoa	50705071
Millennium Golem	47986555

CARD	PASSWORD
Millennium Shield	32012841
Milus Radiant	07489323
Minar	32539892
Minomushi Warrior	46864967
Mirror Force	44095762
Mirror Wall	22359980
Misairuzame	33178416
Molten Destruction	19384334
Monster Egg	36121917
Monster Eye	84133008
Monster Reborn	83764718
Monster Tamer	97612389
Monstrous Bird	35712107
Moon Envoy	45909477
Mooyan Curry	58074572
Morinphen	55784832
Morphing Jar	33508719
Morphing Jar #2	79106360
Mother Grizzly	57839750
Mountain	50913601
Mountain Warrior	04931562
Mr. Volcano	31477025
Muka Muka	46657337
Mushroom Man	14181608
Mushroom Man #2	93900406
Musician King	56907389
M-Warrior #1	56342351
M-Warrior #2	92731455
Mysterious Puppeteer	54098121
Mystic Horseman	68516705
Mystic Lamp	98049915
Mystic Plasma Zone	18161786
Mystic Probe	49251811
Mystic Tomato	83011277
Mystical Capture Chain	63515678
Mystical Elf	15025844

CARD	PASSWORD
Mystical Moon	36607978
Mystical Sand	32751480
Mystical Sheep #1	30451366
Mystical Sheep #2	83464209
Mystical Space Typhoon	05318639
Needle Ball	94230224
Needle Worm	81843628
Negate Attack	14315573
Nekogal #1	01761063
Nekogal #2	43352213
Nemuriko	90963488
Neo the Magic Swordsman	50930991
Nimble Momonga	22567609
Niwatori	07805359
Nobleman of Crossout	71044499
Nobleman of Extermination	17449108
Numinous Healer	02130625
Octoberser	74637266
Ocubeam	86088138
Ogre of the Black Shadow	45121025
One-Eyed Shield Dragon	33064647
Ooguchi	58861941
Ookazi	19523799
Orion the Battle King	02971090
Oscillo Hero	82065276
Oscillo Hero #2	27324313
Painful Choice	74191942
Pale Beast	21263083
Panther Warrior	42035044
Paralyzing Potion	50152549
Parasite Paracide	27911549
Parrot Dragon	62762898
Patrol Robo	76775123
Peacock	20624263
Pendulum Machine	24433920
Penguin Knight	36039163

CARD	PASSWORD
Penguin Soldier	93920745
Petit Angel	38142739
Petit Dragon	75356564
Petit Moth	58192742
Polymerization	24094653
Pot of Greed	55144522
Power of Kaishin	77027445
Pragtical	33691040
Premature Burial	70828912
Prevent Rat	00549481
Princess of Tsurugi	51371017
Prisman	80234301
Prohibition	43711255
Protector of the Throne	10071456
Psychic Kappa	07892180
Pumpking the King of Ghosts	29155212
Punished Eagle	74703140
Queen Bird	73081602
Queen of Autumn Leaves	04179849
Queen's Double	05901497
Raigeki	12580477
Raimei	56260110
Rainbow Flower	21347810
Raise Body Heat	51267887
Rare Fish	80516007
Ray & Temperature	85309439
Reaper of the Cards	33066139
Red Archery Girl	65570596
Red Medicine	38199696
Red-Eyes Black Dragon	74677422
Red-Eyes Black Metal Dragon	64335804
Reinforcements	17814387
Relinquished	64631466
Remove Trap	51482758
Respect Play	08951260
Restructer Revolution	99518961

CARD	PASSWORD
Reverse Trap	77622396
Rhaimundos of the Red Sword	62403074
Right Arm of the Forbidden One	70903634
Right Leg of the Forbidden One	08124921
Ring of Magnetism	20436034
Riryoku	34016756
Rising Air Current	45778932
Roaring Ocean Snake	19066538
Robbin' Goblin	88279736
Rock Ogre Grotto #1	68846917
Rogue Doll	91939608
Root Water	39004808
Rose Spectre of Dunn	32485271
Royal Decree	51452091
Royal Guard	39239728
Rude Kaiser	26378150
Rush Recklessly	70046172
Ryu-Kishin	15303296
Ryu-Kishin Powered	24611934
Ryu-Ran	02964201
Saber Slasher	73911410
Saggi the Dark Clown	66602787
Salamandra	32268901
Sand Stone	73051941
Sangan	26202165
Sea Kamen	71746462
Sea King Dragon	23659124
Seal of the Ancients	97809599
Sebek's Blessing	22537443
Sectarian of Secrets	15507080
Senju of the Thousand Hands	23401839
Seven Tools of the Bandit	03819470
Shadow Specter	40575313
Share the Pain	56830749
Shield & Sword	52097679
Shining Fairy	95956346

CARD	PASSWORD
Shovel Crusher	71950093
Silver Bow and Arrow	01557499
Silver Fang	90357090
Sinister Serpent	08131171
Skelengel	60694662
Skelgon	32355828
Skull Dice	00126218
Skull Red Bird	10202894
Skull Servant	32274490
Skull Stalker	54844990
Skullbird	08327462
Sleeping Lion	40200834
Slot Machine	03797883
Snake Fang	00596051
Snakeyashi	29802344
Snatch Steal	45986603
Sogen	86318356
Solemn Judgment	41420027
Solitude	84794011
Solomon's Lawbook	23471572
Sonic Bird	57617178
Sonic Maid	38942059
Soul Hunter	72869010
Soul of the Pure	47852924
Soul Release	05758500
Sparks	76103675
Spear Cretin	58551308
Spellbinding Circle	18807108
Spike Seadra	85326399
Spirit of the Books	14037717
Spirit of the Harp	80770678
Stain Storm	21323861
Star Boy	08201910
Steel Ogre Grotto #1	29172562
Steel Ogre Grotto #2	90908427
Steel Scorpion	13599884

CARD	PASSWORD
Steel Shell	02370081
Stim-Pack	83225447
Stone Armadiller	63432835
Stone Ogre Grotto	15023985
Stop Defense	63102017
Stuffed Animal	71068263
Succubus Knight	55291359
Summoned Skull	70781052
Supporter in the Shadows	41422426
Swamp Battleguard	40453765
Sword Arm of Dragon	13069066
Sword of Dark Destruction	37120512
Sword of Deep-Seated	98495314
Sword of Dragon's Soul	61405855
Swords of Revealing Light	72302403
Swordsman from a Foreign Land	85255550
Swordstalker	50005633
Tailor of the Fickle	43641473
Tainted Wisdom	28725004
Takriminos	44073668
Takuhee	03170832
Tao the Chanter	46247516
Temple of Skulls	00732302
Tenderness	57935140
Terra the Terrible	63308047
The 13th Grave	00032864
The Bewitching Phantom Thief	24348204
The Bistro Butcher	71107816
The Cheerful Coffin	41142615
The Drdek	08944575
The Eye of Truth	34694160
The Flute of Summoning Dragon	43973174
The Forceful Sentry	42829885
The Furious Sea King	18710707
The Immortal of Thunder	84926738
The Inexperienced Spy	81820689

CARD	PASSWORD
The Little Swordsman of Aile	25109950
The Regulation of Tribe	00296499
The Reliable Guardian	16430187
The Shallow Grave	43434803
The Snake Hair	29491031
The Stern Mystic	87557188
The Thing That Hides in the Mud	18180762
The Unhappy Maiden	51275027
The Wandering Doomed	93788854
The Wicked Worm Beast	06285791
Three-Headed Geedo	78423643
Three-Legged Zombies	33734439
Thunder Dragon	31786629
Tiger Axe	49791927
Time Machine	80987696
Time Seal	35316708
Time Wizard	71625222
Toad Master	62671448
Togex	33878931
Toll	82003859
Tomozaurus	46457856
Tongyo	69572024
Toon Alligator	59383041
Toon Mermaid	65458948
Toon Summoned Skull	91842653
Toon World	15259703
Torike	80813021
Total Defense Shogun	75372290
Trakadon	42348802
Trap Hole	04206964
Trap Master	46461247
Trent	78780140
Trial of Nightmare	77827521
Tribute to the Doomed	79759861
Tripwire Beast	45042329
Turtle Tiger	37313348

CARD	PASSWORD
Twin Long Rods #2	29692206
Twin-Headed Fire Dragon	78984772
Twin-Headed Thunder Dragon	54752875
Two-Headed King Rex	94119974
Two-Mouth Darkruler	57305373
Two-Pronged Attack	83887306
Tyhone	72842870
Tyhone #2	56789759
UFO Turtle	60806437
Ultimate Offering	80604091
Umi	22702055
Umiiruka	82999629
Unknown Warrior of Fiend	97360116
Upstart Goblin	70368879
Uraby	01784619
Ushi Oni	48649353
Valkyrion the Magna Warrior	75347539
Vermillion Sparrow	35752363
Versago the Destroyer	50259460
Vile Germs	39774685
Violent Rain	94042337
Violet Crystal	15052462
Vishwar Randi	78556320
Vorse Raider	14898066
Waboku	12607053
Wall of Illusion	13945283
Warrior Elimination	90873992
Warrior of Tradition	56413937
Wasteland	23424603
Water Element	03732747
Water Girl	55014050
Water Magician	93343894
Water Omotics	02483611
Waterdragon Fairy	66836598
Weather Control	37243151
Weather Report	72053645

CARD	PASSWORD
Whiptail Crow	91996584
White Hole	43487744
White Magical Hat	15150365
Wicked Mirror	15150371
Widespread Ruin	77754944
Windstorm of Etaqua	59744639
Wing Egg Elf	98582704
Winged Cleaver	39175982
Winged Dragon, Guardian of the Fortress #1	87796900
Wings of Wicked Flame	92944626
Witch of the Black Forest	78010363
Witch's Apprentice	80741828
Witty Phantom	36304921
Wodan the Resident of the Forest	42883273
Wood Remains	17733394
World Suppression	12253117
Wow Warrior	69750536
Wretched Ghost of the Attic	17238333
Yado Karu	29380133
Yaiba Robo	10315429
Yamatano Dragon Scroll	76704943
Yami	59197169
Yaranzo	71280811
Zanki	30090452
Zoa	24311372
Zombie Warrior	31339260
Zone Eater	86100785

GAMECUBE™ & GAME BOY® ADVANCE SECRET CODES 2005, VOLUME 1

BradyGames®
An Imprint of Pearson Education
201 West 103rd Street
Indianapolis, Indiana 46290

Please be advised that the ESRB rating icons, "E", "K-A", "T", "M", and "AO" are copyrighted works and certification marks owned by the Interactive Digital Software Association and the Entertainment Software Rating Board and may only be used with their permission and authority. Under no circumstances may the rating icons be self-applied to any product that has not been rated by the ESRB. For information regarding whether a product has been rated by the ESRB, please call the ESRB at (212) 759-0700 or 1-800-771-3772. Please note that ESRB ratings only apply to the content of the game itself and do NOT apply to the content of the books.

ISBN: 0-7440-0490-X

Printing Code: The rightmost double-digit number is the year of the book's printing; the rightmost single-digit number is the number of the book's printing. For example, 04-1 shows that the first printing of the book occurred in 2004.

07 06 05 04   4 3 2 1

Manufactured in the United States of America.

BradyGAMES Staff

Publisher
DAVID WAYBRIGHT

Editor-In-Chief
H. LEIGH DAVIS

Licensing Manager
MIKE DEGLER

Creative Director
ROBIN LASEK

Marketing Director
STEVE ESCALANTE

Marketing Manager
JANET ESHENOUR

Book Credits

Project Editor
HEIDI L. DAVIS

Book Designer
KURT OWENS

Production Designer
JEFF WEISSENBERGER